A GUIDE TO THE STUDY OF GRECO-ROMAN AND JEWISH AND CHRISTIAN HISTORY AND LITERATURE

Philip Walker Jacobs

UNIVERSITY
PRESS OF
AMERICA

Lanham • New York • London

Copyright © 1994 by
University Press of America®, Inc.
4720 Boston Way
Lanham, Maryland 20706

3 Henrietta Street
London WC2E 8LU England

Library of Congress Cataloging-in-Publication Data
Jacobs, Philip Walker.
A guide to the study of Greco-Roman and Jewish and Christian
history and literature / Philip Walker Jacobs.
p.   cm.
Includes bibliographical references and indexes.
1. History, Ancient—Chronology.   I. Title.
D54.5.J33   1994   930—dc20   94–9218 CIP

ISBN 0–8191–9517–0 (pbk. : alk. paper)

 The paper used in this publication meets the minimum requirements of
American National Standard for Information Sciences—Permanence
of Paper for Printed Library Materials, ANSI Z39.48–1984.

To Jane and Thomas and Anna,

"You are the salt of the earth . . . .
You are the light of the world."

Contents

Sigla and Abbreviations

o   A small circle placed next to a literary work indicates that the work is extant.

B.C.E.   Before Common Era

C.E.   Common Era

Preface

Since my earliest days as a student of ancient history and religion, I have been aware of the need for a reference tool which could enable both the student of religion and the student of ancient history to better understand the broad context of social and religious development in the Hellenistic world. The present text represents my response to this need. The purpose of this guide is to provide students of ancient history, literature, and religion with a reference guide that will enable them to better understand the broad context of social and religious development in the Hellenistic world in the period between 200 BCE and 260 CE. Thus, the focus of this work is on persons, groups, movements, events, and literature that influenced political, social, religious, literary, and philosophical developments in the Hellenistic world.

The text is divided into two main sections: Greco-Roman History and Literature and Jewish and Christian History and Literature. In the Greco-Roman History and Literature section the expansion of territory; rebellion and strife; social and political developments; emperors, consuls, rulers, and other important political figures; literary figures and literature; and the rise and influence of philosophical teachers and schools of philosophy and of religions and cults within the Republic and the Empire are noted. In the Jewish and Christian History and Literature section personalities, groups, and movements in Judaism and the early church; the literature of Judaism and Christianity; the persecution of Jews and Christians and other religious and philosophical groups; Roman rule and influence in Syria-Palestine, and the rule and influence of other nations and groups in Syria-Palestine are noted.

Certainty often eludes the student of ancient history and religion. While some dates in this chronology can be established with great certainty many cannot. It is necessary to come to conclusions on the basis of limited evidence. In numerous instances dates have been established in this chronology on the basis of very limited evidence. Nonetheless, in these cases, I believe historical tradition and scholarly opinion have provided a basis for the placement of a particular person or event or literary work in a general period, if not at a specific time.

Though this text has been carefully checked for omissions and errors, I am well aware of the possibility for both, and thus, would welcome suggestions and corrections from the readers of this text.

Acknowledgments

In my intellectual and spiritual journey, I have been blessed by the contributions of numerous individuals.

My own late father and my mother and D. Elton Trueblood of Earlham College provided the earliest intellectual stimulation and challenge for me.

Their special contributions have been complemented over the years by John Jackson of Southern Illinois University; Paul Achtemeier, John Carroll, James Mays, Matthias Rissi, and James Smylie of Union Theological Seminary in Virginia; Paul Barolsky, Harry Gamble, David Kovacs and Judy Kovacs of the University of Virginia; Bruce Metzger, now emeritus of Princeton Theological Seminary; Christopher Thomas of the Church of God School of Theology; James Buchanan, now emeritus of Tulane University; and my beloved wife, Jane.

Each of these individuals has been generous and gracious to me in their review and criticism of my academic work. Without their assistance this work would never have come to fruition.

A GUIDE TO THE
STUDY OF GRECO-ROMAN AND
JEWISH AND CHRISTIAN
HISTORY AND LITERATURE

JEWISH AND CHRISTIAN HISTORY AND LITERATURE

**200
BCE**   Antiochus III, Seleucid King of Syria, defeats Egyptians at Panium. Antiochus III rules Palestine and Syria until 187. (200)

Ecclesiasticus°* (The Wisdom of Jesus the Son of Sirach) (200-175),
I Enoch°, chapters 1-36, (200-150),
Sibylline Oracles°, Book III, (200-100),
Martyrdom of Isaiah° (200-100),
I Enoch , chapters 92-105, (200-40) written. (200)

Seleucus IV, Seleucid King, rules Syria and Palestine, 187-176. (187)

**187
BCE**

---

* The symbol° next to an ancient text indicates that this text is extant.

GRECO-ROMAN HISTORY AND LITERATURE

Second Macedonian War between Romans and Macedonians, **200**
200-196. (200)   **BCE**

Macedonians under Philip defeated. Peace settlement between
Macedonians and Romans. Antiochus at Ephesus. (197)

P. Terentius Afer (195-159) born. Latin comic poet. *Andria°*
(*The Lady of Andros*), *Heauton Timoumenos°*, (*Self-
Tormentor*), *Eunuchus* (*The Eunuch*). (195)

Exiled Hannibal united with Antiochus. (195)

Romans leave Greece. (194)

Antiochus in Greece. (192)

Romans conduct war against Antiochus, 192-189. (192)

Antiochus defeated in Greece; retreats to Asia Minor. Defeat of
Antiochus' fleet off Asia Minor. (191)

Antiochus' fleet again defeated. (190)

Defeat of Antiochus in Greece. (190-189)

Cato, censor. (184)

Hannibal dies. (183)
                                                    183
                                                    BCE

JEWISH AND CHRISTIAN HISTORY AND LITERATURE

**176
BCE**

Antiochus IV (Epiphanes), Seleucid King, rules Syria and Palestine, 176-163. (176)

Onias dismissed as High Priest of Jews. (176)

Jason, High Priest of Jews, 175-171. (175)

"Hellenization" of Jerusalem, under Seleucid direction, begins. (175)

Book of Jubilees°, (175-100), and *The Testament of Moses°* *(The Assumption of Moses)* (175 BCE-40 CE) written. (175)

Jason dismissed as High Priest. (172)

Menelaus, High Priest of Jews, 171-162. (171)

Daniel° (170-165), *Zechariah 9-14°*, *Testament of Levi°*, *Testament of Naphtali°*, (170-130) written. (170)

Antiochus IV plunders Jerusalem temple. (168)

Antiochus IV stopped by Romans in his second campaign against Egypt. He and his supporters prohibit the practice of Jewish religion under threat of death. Jewish temple at Jerusalem is turned into temple of Olympian Zeus. (167)

Maccabees (Jewish priests and fighters) under Mattathias and Judas Maccabaeus lead revolt against Antiochus IV. (167)

**166
BCE** Mattathias Maccabaeus dies. (166)

GRECO-ROMAN HISTORY AND LITERATURE

Rebellion in Corsica and Sardinia. First Celtiberian War 181-   **181**
179. Tiberius Gracchus pacifies Celtiberians. (181)   **BCE**

Sardinia destroyed. (177-176)

Expulsion of two Epicurean philosophers in Rome. (173)

Third Macedonian War. (172-167)

Macedonian war ends. Macedonia is divided into four
republics; Illyricum is divided into three protectorates. (167)

167
BCE

JEWISH AND CHRISTIAN HISTORY AND LITERATURE

165 BCE   Judas Maccabaeus, leader of Judah, 165-160. (165)

Judith° (165-40) written. (165)

Jews reconsecrate Jerusalem temple. Inauguration of Jewish religious celebration of Hannukah. (164)

Baruch° (164-120) written. (164)

Antiochus IV dies, and is succeeded by Antiochus V (Eupator) who rules Syria and Palestine, 163-161. (163)

Antiochus V (Eupator) campaigns against Maccabees and defeats Judas Maccabaeus. (163)

Treaty of peace established between Maccabees and Seleucids. (162)

Alcimus, High Priest of Jews, 162-159. (162)

Judas Maccabaeus establishes alliance with Rome. (161)

Demetrius I (Soter), Seleucid King, rules Syria and Palestine from 161-150. (161)

Judas Maccabaeus dies. Succeeded by Jonathan Maccabaeus who rules Judah, 160-142. (160)

Qumran (Dead Sea) community of Essenes established 160 and continues in existence until 68 CE. Qumran Literature: *The Community Rule° (The Manual of Discipline), The Damascus Rule°, The Messianic Rule°, The War Rule°, Hymns Scroll°,* and numerous works of commentary on Jewsih scriptures, 160-68 CE. (160)

160 BCE   *I Enoch°*, chapters 83-90, written. (160)

GRECO-ROMAN HISTORY AND LITERATURE

163
BCE

Corsica destroyed. (163)

Greek philosophers expelled. Treaty established with Jews. (161)

Lusitanian War, (154-138).　　**154**
BCE

JEWISH AND CHRISTIAN HISTORY AND LITERATURE

153 BCE Alexander Balas establishes himself as rival to Seleucid throne against Demetrius I for a year. (153)

Jonathan Maccabaeus, Judean ruler, becomes Jewish High Priest. (152)

Alexander Balas, Seleucid King, rules Syria and Palestine, 150-145. (150)

Demetrius II (Nicator), Seleucid King, rules Syria and Palestine, 145-138. Tryphon, Seleucid political leader, establishes Antiochus VI, a minor, as a rival to Demetrius II for Seleucid throne. Antiochus VI rules as rival, 145-143. (145)

Tryphon continues rule of opposition to Demetrius II, 143-138. (143)

Jonathan Maccabaeus dies. Simon Maccabaeus succeeds him as ruler and High Priest of Judah and rules, 142-134. (142)

Jews win complete independence from Seleucid rule and conquer Ancra. (142)

Antiochus VII, Seleucid King, rules Syria, 138-129. (138)

Letter of Aristeas° (135-100) written. (135)

135 BCE

GRECO-ROMAN HISTORY AND LITERATURE

Second Celtiberian War. (153-151)   **153**
                                                     BCE

Third Punic War. Carthage under siege. (149-146)

Scipio Aemilianus directs siege of Carthage. Macedonia made Roman province. (147)

Carthage destroyed. Africa made province. War with Achaeans. Corinth destroyed. (146)

Third Celtiberian War. (143-133)

Scipio Aemilianus, censor. (142)

Sicilian Slave War. (135-132)

Posidonius (135-51) active. Stoic philosopher, instructor to Cicero. *Histories.*

                                                     135
                                                     BCE

JEWISH AND CHRISTIAN HISTORY AND LITERATURE

134 BCE Jews enter a prosperous period. Simon Maccabaeus dies. John Hyrcanus, Simon's son becomes ruler of Judah and rules, 134-104. Antiochus VII conquers Jerusalem and grants it autonomy. (134)

Demetrius II (Nicator), again, Seleucid King, rules, 129-125. (129)

Samaritan temple on Mt. Gerizim destroyed by John Hyrcanus. (128)

Seleucus V, Seleucid King, for a short time. Immediately followed by Antiochus VIII, Seleucid King, who rules Syria, 125-113. (125)

125 BCE

GRECO-ROMAN HISTORY AND LITERATURE

**133
BCE**

Scipio Aemilianus destroys Numantia; takes Spain. (133)

Scipio Aemilianus dies. Organization of Asian province. (129)

Strife in Sardinia. (126)

Franchisement of Latins proposed by consul Fulvius Flaccus. Fregellae rebels. (125)

War in Gaul against Arverni and Allobroges. (124-121)

Gaius Gracchus, tribune; reelected in 122. (123)

Gaius Gracchus, opposed by Livius Drusus. (122)

Civil strife. Gracchus killed. Consul, L. Opimius, executes followers of Gracchus. (121)

Arverni and Allobroges defeated. (121)

Marius, tribune. Gracchan land commission annulled. (119)

Polybius (204-117), Greek historian, dies. Authored forty books that recorded the history of the ancient world from 220-146 BCE. *The Histories*°. (117)

**117
BCE**

JEWISH AND CHRISTIAN HISTORY AND LITERATURE

113
BCE

Antiochus IX, Seleucid heir, rules Syria, 113-111. (113)

Antiochus IX rules Coele-Syria (region south of Syria), 111-95. Antiochus VIII, former Seleucid King, returns to power and rules as Seleucid King over Syria, 111-96.(111)

111
BCE

GRECO-ROMAN HISTORY AND LITERATURE

Varro (M. Terentius) (116-27) born. Latin "renaissance man". **116** Politician, philosopher, grammarian, poet, and satirist. He **BCE** authored over six-hundred volumes. *De Re Rustica° (On Agriculture)*, and two volumes of *De Lingua Latina° (On The Latin Language)* extant. (116)

Aemilius Scaurus, consul. (115)

Marius in Spain. (114)

Q. Hortensius (114-50) born. Latin rhetorician and politician. Member of aristocratic party. Praetor and consul with Q. Caecilius Metellius in 69. (114)

Jugurtha ransacks Cirta in Numidia. Rome declares war on Jugurtha. (112)

Jugurthine War. (112-105)

Pact with Jugurtha. (111)

African war; Aulus Albinus surrenders. (110) Jugurtha continues fighting. (109)

Cicero (M. Tullus Cicero) (106-43) born. Latin rhetorician and philosopher and politician. Consul, 63. Banished and recalled in 57. Aside from fifty-eight orations, Cicero's extant works include *De Oratore° (The Making Of An Orator)*, *De Re Publica° (The Republic)*, *De Legibus° (The Laws)*, *De Officiis° (Moral Duties)*, *De Senectute° (An Old Age)*, *De Divinatione° (Divination)* and *De Amicitia° (On Friendship)*. (106)

Roman armies destroyed by Cimbri and Teutones. (105) **105**
BCE

JEWISH AND CHRISTIAN HISTORY AND LITERATURE

**104
BCE**

Judas Aristobulus I, son of John Hyrcanus, reinstitutes kingship in Judea, and establishes himself as king; shortly afterwards he dies. (104)

I Maccabees° (104-63) written. (104)

Alexander Jannaeus, brother of Aristobulus I, rules as King and High Priest, 103-76. During his rule he persecutes the Pharisees. (103)

II Maccabees° (103-76) written.

Susanna°, *Bel and the Dragon*°, *The Prayer of Azariah and the Song of the Three Young Men*° (additions to *Daniel*), and *Esther* additions (100-50) written. (100)

III Maccabees° (100-1) and *II Enoch*° (100-1) written.(100)

**100
BCE**

GRECO-ROMAN HISTORY AND LITERATURE

Marius, consul for second time; he reorganizes Roman army. (104)   **104**
BCE
Second Sicilian slave war. (104-101)

Land allotments given to veterans of Marius' army. Marius, again, consul. (103)

Marius, consul for fourth time; subdues Teutones. (102)

Marius, consul for fifth time. Cimbri defeated by Romans. (101)

C. Julius Caesar (100-44) born. Famous Latin statesman, consul, soldier, dictator, historian. Assassinated in 44. *Commentari*—ten books of history, *Bellum Civile°* (*The Civil Wars*), *De Bello Alexandrino°* (*The Alexandrian War*), *De Bello Africo°* (*The African War*), *De Bello Hispaniensi°* (*The Spanish War*) and, *De Bello Gallico°* (*The Gallic War*). (100)

Marius, consul for sixth. He restores order after riots erupt in Rome. (100)

Marius in Asia. (98)

Lucretius (T. Lucretius Carus) (98-55) born. Latin poet. Epicurean. He authored *De Rerum Natura°* (*On The Nature of Things*), a philosophical poem that explicates Epicureanism. (98)

Sulla, praetor.   **98**
BCE

JEWISH AND CHRISTIAN HISTORY AND LITERATURE

95 BCE   Antiochus X, Seleucid King, rules Syria, 95-83. (95)

83 BCE   Tigranes I, King of Armenia, rules Syria and Phoenicia, 83-69. (83)

GRECO-ROMAN HISTORY AND LITERATURE

Tigranes, King of Armenia. (95)   **95 BCE**

Cato (M. Porcius Cato, Cato Uticensus) (95-46) born. Latin orator and philosopher. Stoic. Leader in aristocratic party. Committed suicide. *De Agri Cultura°* (*On Agriculture*). (95)

Censors suppress Latin rhetors. (92)

Social war begins. (91)

Continuation of Social War. (90)

Pompeius Strabo and Sulla victorious. (89)

Sulpicius Rufus, tribune. Rome seized by Sulla. Escape of Marius. Asia overrun by Mithridates.

Rome taken by Cinna and Marius. Sulla's supporters massacred. Sulla in Greece. Cinna, consul, 87-84. (87)

Sallust (C. Sallustius Crispus) (86-34) born. Latin historian and politician. *Bellum Catilinae°*, (*The War With Catiline*) and *Bellum Jugurthinum°* (*The War With Jugurtha*). (86)

Marius consul for seventh time. Death of Marius. (86)

Athens captured by Sulla. Mithridates defeated by Sulla. (86)

Treaty pact made with Mithridates. (85)

Cinna murdered. Carbo, consul. (84)

Catullus (Valerius Catullus) (84-54) born. Latin poet. *Veronensis Liber°* (*The Poems*).

Italy invaded by Sulla. Pompey supports Sulla. (83)   **83 BCE**

JEWISH AND CHRISTIAN HISTORY AND LITERATURE

**80
BCE**

Psalms of Solomon° (80-20) written. (80)

Salome Alexandra, Hasmonean queen, rules Judea, 76-67. (76)

Hyrcanus II is High Priest of Jews, 76-40. (76)

**76
BCE**

GRECO-ROMAN HISTORY AND LITERATURE

Italian civil war. Victory of Sulla. (82)

Second Mithridatic War. (81)
Sulla dictator. Marius defeated by Pompey in Africa. (81)

Sulla introduces goddess Ma to Roman peoples (a divinity from Asia Minor [Anatolia], associated with goddess Cybele, goddess of war). (81-80)

Sulla abrogates dictatorship. (79)

Death of Sulla. (78)

Cyrene becomes Roman province. Bithynia invaded by Mithridates. (74)

Rebellion of slaves led by Spartacus in Italy. Mithridates defeated by Lucullus. (73)

Spartacus' victories. (72)

Spartacus defeated by Crassus. Mithridates again defeated by Lucullus. Mithridates flees to Tigranes. (71)

Pompey and Crassus, co-consuls; tribunician powers restored. (70)

Virgil (P. Vergilius Maro) (70-19) born. Latin epic poet. *Eclogues°*, *Georgics°*, *The Aeneid°*, and several other extant poems. (70)

**82
BCE**

**70
BCE**

JEWISH AND CHRISTIAN HISTORY AND LITERATURE

69
BCE   Antiochus XII, Seleucid King, rules Syria, 69-65. (69)

Hyrcanus II, King of Judea, for a brief time. (67)

Aristobulus II, King of Judea, 66-63. (66)

Scaurus, Roman military general, serves as legate of Syria. (65)

Pompey, military commander of Roman forces in East, enters Syria and ends Seleucid rule in Syria-Palestine. (64)

Pompey ends resistance in Palestine by capturing Jerusalem; violates Temple by entering "holy of holies". Judea incorporated into Roman province of Syria. (63)

Antipator (Antipas), father of Herod I (Herod the Great), cooperates with Romans in their administration of Judea, 63-43. (63)

Scaurus, again, Roman legate of Syria. (62)

62
BCE

GRECO-ROMAN HISTORY AND LITERATURE

Armenia invaded by Lucullus. (69)

**69
BCE**

Pontus again invaded by Mithridates. (68)

Pirates in Mediterranean defeated by Pompey. (67)

Mithridates' forces defeated by Pompey. (66)

Pompey continues his pursuit of Mithridates and fights in Caucasus. (65)

Horace (Q. Horatius Flaccus) (65-8) born. Latin poet. *Sermonum° (Satires), Epistularum° (Epistles)*, and *De Arte Poetica° (The Art of Poetry)*. (65)

Pompey in Syria. Seleucid influence in Syria-Palestine ended. (64)

Cicero, consul. Pompey in Jerusalem. Mithridates dies. (63)

Eastern situation resolved by Pompey; Syria made Roman province. (62)

Triumph of Pompey. Julius Caesar designated governor of Further Spain. (61)

Caesar returns from Spain; pact with Pompey and Crassus. First Triumvirate established. (60)

Roman Senate orders destruction of altars and statues of Isis and Serapis. (59)

**59
BCE**

JEWISH AND CHRISTIAN HISTORY AND LITERATURE

**57
BCE**

Galbinius, Roman legate of Syria, 57-55. (57)

Crassus, member of triumvir, rules as Roman legate of Syria, 55-53. (55)

**55
BCE**

GRECO-ROMAN HISTORY AND LITERATURE

Caesar, consul. (59)   **59**
                                                                        BCE

Livy (T. Livius) (59-17 CE) born. Latin historian. His greatest
work is his history of Rome which covers the period from the
founding of Rome to 9 BCE in 142 books. Thirty-five books in
this history are extant. *Ab Urbe Condita°* (*From The Founding
of the City*). (59)

Cicero exiled. Helvetii and Ariovistus defeated by Caesar.
Ptolemy forced out of Alexandria. (58)

Strabo (58-24 CE) born. Greek geographer and historian.
Geography°. (58)

Roman Senate, again, orders destruction of altars and statues of
Isis and Serapis. (58)

Return of Cicero. Belgae and Nervii defeated by Caesar. (57)

Conflict among triumvirs. Caesar fights Veneti and Morini.
(56)

Pompey and Crassus hold second consulship. Usipetes and
Tencteri destroyed by Caesar. Britain invaded by Caesar. (55)

Seneca the Elder (M. Annaeus Seneca) (55-40 CE) born.
Rhetorician and author. *Controversiae°* (*Controversies*) and
Suasoriarum° (*The Suasoriae*). (55)

Rome riots. Caesar gains in Britain. (54)

Sextus Propertius (54-15) born. Latin poet. Admitted to the
literary circle of Maecenas. Acquainted with Ovid and other
prominent contemporary literary figures. Four books of love
poems addressed to his purported mistress are extant.
Elegiarum° (*The Elegies*). (54)

                                                                        54
                                                                        BCE

JEWISH AND CHRISTIAN HISTORY AND LITERATURE

53   Crassus, defeated and killed by Parthians. Cassius replaces
BCE   Crassus as Roman governor in Syria and rules from 53-51. (53)

Letter of Jeremiah° (Hebrew), *Prayer of Manasseh°, The Apocalypse of Moses°, Life of Adam and Eve°, Joseph and Aseneth°,* and *III Ezra° (I Esdras)* (50 BCE-50 CE) written. (50)

Julius Caesar, military commander of Roman forces in East, 48-46. (48)

Hyrcanus II, ethnarch (King) of Palestine; rules in cooperation with Romans from 47-40. (47)

**47
BCE**

GRECO-ROMAN HISTORY AND LITERATURE

Rome riots. Parthians defeat and kill Crassus. (53)

**53
BCE**

Roman Senate, again, orders destruction of altars and statues of Isis and Serapis. (53)

Syria invaded by Parthians. (51)

Pompey asked to save state by Marcellus. (50)

Caesar organizes in Gaul and crosses the Rubicon into Italy. Civil war begins. Pompey flees to Greece. Caesar, dictator. Pompeians defeated by Caesar in Spain. (49)

Caesar consul for second time. Pompey defeated by Caesar in Greece; later killed in Egypt. (48)

Tibullus (Albius Tibullus) (48-19) born. Latin poet. Wrote several romantic elegies which are extant. *The Poems°*. (48)

Roman Senate, again, orders destruction of altars and statues of Isis and Serapis. (48)

Caesar dictator for second time. Caesar leaves Egypt, returns to Italy, settles internal disturbances. (47)

Pompeians defeated in Africa by Caesar. Caesar, still dictator, becomes consul for third time; triumphs in Rome. (46)

Caesar reestablishes Corinth as Colonia Julia Corinthus for veterans of the Roman army. (46)

Caesar becomes dictator for third time and consul for fourth time. Pompeians defeated by Caesar in Spain. Caesar returns to Rome. (45)

**45
BCE**

JEWISH AND CHRISTIAN HISTORY AND LITERATURE

44   Cassius serves as military commander of Roman forces in East
BCE   from 44-42. (44)

Phasael and Herod the Great, generals of Judean armies, fight
with Romans, 43-40. (43)

Antony, military commander of Roman forces in East, 41-31.
(41)

Antigonus, King of Judea, rules in cooperation with Romans,
40-37. (40)

Herod I (Herod the Great), King of Judea, rules in cooperation
with Romans, 37-4. (37)

Ananel (of Babylon), High Priest of Jews, 37-36. (37)

37
BCE

GRECO-ROMAN HISTORY AND LITERATURE

Caesar confirmed as dictator for life; consul for fifth time. **44** Caesar murdered in conspiracy. Octavian returns from Greece. **BCE** Antony commands army in Gaul (44)

Ovid (P. Ovidius Naso) (43-18CE) born. Latin poet. Banished in 8 CE. He authored *Metamorphoses°, Fasti°, Tristia°, Ex-Ponto°, Heroides°, Amores°, Ars Amatoria°* and several other extant poems. (43)

Triumvirs build temple in honor of Isis, female Egyptian goddess. (43)

Hirtius and Pansa, consuls, killed. D. Brutus killed. Octavian made consul. Triumvirate of Antony, Octavian, and Lepidus created. Proscriptions. Cicero executed. M. Brutus in Macedonia. Cassius in Syria. (43) Julius Caesar made Divus. Brutus and Cassius defeated in Greece (Philippi) by Antony. (42)

Antony in Asia Minor. Meets Cleopatra and visits Alexandria. (41)

Agreement between Antony, Octavius, and Lepidus at Brundisium divides the Roman world among the three triumvirate leaders. Parthians invade Syria and eventually overtake Judea. Herod the Great recognized by Roman Senate as King of Judea. (40)

Antony, Octavian, and Sextus Pompeius reach agreement at Misenum. Parthians defeated by Ventidius. (39)

Triumvirate continued. Herod the Great and C. Sosius (Antony's Lieutenant) capture Jerusalem from Parthians. Herod reigns over Judea. Antony marries Cleopatra at Antioch. (37)

37
BCE

JEWISH AND CHRISTIAN HISTORY AND LITERATURE

35
BCE

Aristobulus III, High Priest of Jews. (35)

Ananel, again, High Priest of Jews. (34)

34
BCE

GRECO-ROMAN HISTORY AND LITERATURE

Triumvirate dissolves. Octavian attacks and defeats Sextus   **36**
Pompeius. Antony retreats through Armenia. (36)   **BCE**

Antony invades Armenia; celebrates his victory in Alexandria.
(34)

Antony in Armenia. Octavian, again, consul. (33-32)

Antony in Greece. (32-31)

Octavian, again, consul. His tenure lasts until 23. (31)

Octavian defeats Antony at Actium; winters in Asia. (31)

Tribunician power bestowed on Octavian. Antony and
Cleopatra commit suicide as Octavian enters Alexandria. (30)

Octavian's triumph. Temple of Divus Julius dedicated. (29)

Octavian and Agrippa hold census. Temple of Apollo on
Palatine is dedicated by Octavian. (28)

Octavian Augustus (Augustus Caesar) becomes first Roman
emperor and rules from 27 BCE until his death in 14 CE. (27)

Period known as "the Principate" begins. Octavian, now called
Augustus, given imperium for ten years. Augustus in Gaul and
Spain till 25 BCE. (27)

In concord with Emperor Augustus' disdain of Egyptian
deities, a regulation is passed prohibiting the erection of altars
to Isis and Serapis inside the pomerium. (28)

Aelius Gallus engages in Arabian expedition. (25-24)   **25**
                                                             BCE

JEWISH AND CHRISTIAN HISTORY AND LITERATURE

24   Simon Boethus (of Alexandria), High Priest of Jews, 24-4. (24)
BCE

Agrippa, military commander of Roman forces in East, 23-20.
(23)

Philo (Philo Judeus) (20 BCE-46 CE) born. Alexandrian Greek
Jewish philosopher, politician, and scriptural exegete. *Against
Flaccus°, Embassy to Gaius°, Apology for the Jews°, Life of
Moses°, Contemplative Life°, Exposition of the Law°* (series of
treatises), *Allegory of the Jewish Law°* (series), *Questions and
Answers in Genesis and Exodus°* (series), *On the
Indestructibility of the World°, That Every Virtuous Man Is
Free°, On Providence°, Alexander or On the Question Whether
Dumb Animals Have the Power of Reason°.* (20)

20
BCE

GRECO-ROMAN HISTORY AND LITERATURE

Dionysius of Halicarnassus, Greek historian and literary critic. **23**
Flourished during reign of Augustus Caesar. Dates for his life **BCE**
are unknown. Authored numerous treatises. *Romaikes*
Archaiologias° *(The Roman Antiquities)* and several shorter
exant works.

Petronius conducts Ethiopian War. (23)

Augustus resigns consulship; given imperium proconsular
maius and tribunicia potestas. (22)

Agrippa extends prohibition against the erection of altars to Isis
and Serapis to a radius of a thousand paces around Rome. (21)

Augustus refuses to accept dictatorship and consulship for life;
goes to Greece and Asia for three years. (21-19)

C. Velleius Paterculus (20-30CE) born. Latin historian.
Historiae Romanae° *(The Roman History)*. (20)

Tiberius enters Armenia. (19)

Augustus returns to Rome. Agrippa pacifies Spain. (18)

Imperium of Augustus renewed for five more years. Agrippa **18**
given imperium maius and tribunicia potestas. (18) **BCE**

JEWISH AND CHRISTIAN HISTORY AND LITERATURE

17   Agrippa, again, military commander of Roman forces in East,
BCE   17-13. (17)

Jesus of Nazareth (7 BCE-30 CE) born. Palestinian Jewish prophet and teacher from the region of Galilee. The central historical religious figure in Christianity. He is identified in the Christian scriptures by various titles: "Son of Man," "Son of David," "the prophet," "teacher," "the Galilean," "the Nazarene," "Christ," "Jesus Christ," "Lord," "Savior," and "Son of God." The gospels of *Mark, Matthew, Luke*, and *John* in the Christian *New Testament* contain descriptions of his birth, life, teaching, death, and resurrection. Christians believe Jesus to be the son of God. They believe Jesus ministered on earth (29-30), was crucified (30), and was resurrected from the dead (30) so that all persons may receive the salvation of God. (7)

6   Varus, Roman governor of Syria, 6-3. (6)
BCE

GRECO-ROMAN HISTORY AND LITERATURE

Augustus in Gaul for three years. Agrippa in East. (16)

Defeat of Raeti and Vindelict by Tiberius and Drusus. Forces of Tiberius and Drusus reach the Danube. (15)

Augustus returns from Gaul; his imperium renewed for five years. Tiberius serves as consul. Agrippa returns. (13)

Augustus designated Pontifex Maximus (Chief High Priest). Agrippa dies. Tiberius in Pannonia. (12)

Drusus dies. (9)

Imperium of Augustus renewed for ten years. Census held. Tiberius in Germany. (8)

Maecenas dies. He was a minister and friend of Augustus Caeser. He was also a patron of a literary circle that included Virgil and Horace. (8)

Roman Empire divided into fourteen regions. (7)

Tiberius designated tribunicia potestas for five years. Tiberius takes up residence in seclusion on Rhodes. (6)

JEWISH AND CHRISTIAN HISTORY AND LITERATURE

5
BCE   Civil strife in Palestine. (5)

Herod I (Herod the Great) dies and his authority is divided among his sons. Archelaus, his principal successor, rules as ethnarch (King) of Judea, Samaria, and Idumea, 4 BCE-6 CE. Philip, rules as tetrach of Iturea and Trachonitis, 4 BCE-34 CE.

4   Herod Antipas rules as tetrach of Galilee and Perea, 4 BCE-39
BCE   CE. (4)

1   COMMON ERA
CE
Wisdom of Solomon° (1-50), and *I Enoch°*, chapters 37-71 (1-50) written. (1)

II Enoch° (1-100), and *Testament of Job°* (1-100) written. (1)

Annas (Ananus I), High Priest of Jews, 6-15. (6)

Archelaus, ethnarch (King) of Judea, Samaria and Idumea, is exiled by Romans because of his harsh treatment of Jews and Samaritans. (6)

6   Judea is made a Roman province. Coponius procurator of Judea
CE   and Samaria, 6-9. (6)

GRECO-ROMAN HISTORY AND LITERATURE

Twelfth consulship of Augustus. Augustus' grandson, Gaius   **5**
Caesar, assumes toga virilis. (5)   **BCE**

Herod the Great dies. (4)

Seneca the Younger (L. Annaeus Seneca) (4-65 CE) born. Stoic
philosopher, playwright and statesman. Tutor and minister of
Nero. *Epistulae Morales Ad Lucilium°*, *(The Moral Epistles to
Lucilius)*, *Tragedies°*, *Naturales Quaestiones°* *(Natural
Questions)*, and *Dialogorum ° (The Dialogues* or *Moral
Essays)*. (4)

Augustus consul for thirteenth time; receives title of Pater
Patriae (Father of the Country). Dedication of temple of Mars   **2**
Ultor (Mars the Avenger, the Roman war god). (2)   **BCE**

COMMON ERA
1
CE

Imperium of Gaius Caesar in the East, in Syria. (l)

Augustus' imperium renewed for ten years. (3)

Augustus adopts Tiberius. Tiberius given tribunicia potestas for
ten years. Tiberius adopts Germanicus. Lex Aelia Sentia—
against indiscriminate emancipation of slaves. (4)

Rebellion in Pannonia and Illyricum (6)

6
CE

JEWISH AND CHRISTIAN HISTORY AND LITERATURE

6
CE   P. Sulpicius Quirinius, Roman legate of Syria, rules Syria, 6-11. He conducts census, 6. (6)

Ambibulus, Roman procurator of Judea and Samaria, 9-12. (9)

Rufus, Roman procurator of Judea and Samaria, 12-15. (12)

Valerius Gratus, Roman procurator of Judea and Samaria, 15-26. (15)

Caiaphas, High Priest of Jews, 18-36. (18)

Jews banished from Rome. (19)

IV Maccabees° (20-54) written. (20)

20
CE

GRECO-ROMAN HISTORY AND LITERATURE

Claudius becomes an augur. (8)

Lex Papia Poppaea - penalized celibates and those in childless marriages. (9)

Triumph of Tiberius. (12)

Imperium of Augustus is renewed for ten years. Tiberius given tribunicia potestas and proconsular imperium. (13)

Death of Augustus. Tiberius becomes second Roman emperor and rules from 14 until his death in 37. Rebellion of legions in Pannonia and Germany. Roman absorption of eastern client kings. (14)

Triumph of Germanicus. Germanicus sent to eastern part of Empire. Cn. Calpurnius Piso, formerly consul with Tiberius in 7, appointed legate of Syria. Earthquake in Asia Minor. (17)

Tiberius, consul with Germanicus. Germanicus in east. Germanicus goes to Egypt. (18)

Piso departs from Syria. Death of Germanicus at Antioch. Scandal of Isaic priesthood at Rome. Emperor Tiberius orders persecution of Isaic priests and with aid of Roman Senate expels Jews and followers of Isis. (19)

Tiberius consul with his son Drusus. (21)

JEWISH AND CHRISTIAN HISTORY AND LITERATURE

**26
CE**

Pontius Pilate, Roman procurator of Judea and Samaria, 26-36. (26)

John the Baptizer, active, 28-29. (28)

Jesus of Nazareth, active, 29-30. (29)

Jesus, crucified. Christians believe Jesus of Nazareth was resurrected from the dead three days after his burial. (30)

Beginning of Jewish Christian community in Jerusalem under the direction of James, the brother of Jesus. (30)

Martyrdom of Stephen in Jerusalem. (33)

Hellenistic Christians expelled from Jerusalem. (33)

Beginning of Gentile mission in Judea and Samaria. (33)

Conversion of Saul (Paul the Apostle). (34)

Vitellius, Roman legate of Syria, 35-39. (35)

Marcellus, Roman procurator of Judea and Samaria, 36-41. (36)

**36
CE**   Jonathan, High Priest of Jews, 36-37. (36)

GRECO-ROMAN HISTORY AND LITERATURE

Pliny the Elder (C. Plinius Secundus) (23-79) born. Latin   **23**
politician and historian. *Historia Naturalis° (Natural History).*   **CE**
(23)

Rebellion in Thrace settled. Pontius Pilate made procurator of
Judaea. (26)

Revolt of the Frisii. (28)

Tiberius consul with Sejanus. Gaius given toga virilis. Sejanus
put to death. (31)

Tetrachy of Phillip subsumed into Syria. (34)

Persius (A. Persius Flaccus) (34-62) born. Latin poet. *Persi
Saturae° (The Satires of Persius).* (34)

L. Vitellius, governor of Syria, sends Pilate to Rome because of
his poor administration of Palestine. (36)

**36
CE**

JEWISH AND CHRISTIAN HISTORY AND LITERATURE

37
CE
Marullus, Roman procurator of Judea and Samaria, 37-41. (37)

Theophilus, High Priest of Jews, 37-41. (37)

Josephus (Flavius Josephus, Joseph ben Matthias) (37-100) born. Judean Greek Jewish politician, and historian. He served as governor of Galilee in 66. He was captured by the Romans in 66 during the war between the Jews and the Romans and held in custody for three years. He went to Rome in 70 after Jerusalem fell. There he wrote his political and historical treatises. *The Jewish War*° (seven volumes), *The Life*°, *Antiquities of the Jews*° (twenty volumes covering the history of the Jewish people), and *Against Apion*°. (37)

Therapeutae, Egyptian Jewish monastic sect, who believed in allegorical interpretation of Jewish scriptures and resided near Alexandria and Lake Mareotis, flourish.

Great pogrom against Alexandrian Jews by Gentiles in Alexandria, 37-39. Philo Judeus, Alexandrian Jewish philosopher, heads Jewish delegation to Rome to end pogrom. (37)

Demonstrations against Gaius Caesar (Caligula) in Judea. (39)

Petronius, Roman legate of Syria, 39-42. (39)

40
CE
Anti-Jewish riots in Antioch, Syria. (40)

GRECO-ROMAN HISTORY AND LITERATURE

Death of Tiberius. Gaius Caesar (Caligula) becomes third   **37**
Roman emperor and rules from 37 until his death in 41.   **CE**
Caligula serves as consul with Claudius. (37)

During his reign, Caligula gives permission for worship of Isis.
Rituals of Isis popular throughout empire, particularly among
lower classes.

Death and deification of Drusilla. (38)

Jewish unrest in Alexandria. (38)

Caligula constructs temple for Isis on Campus Martius outside
the sacred enclosure of the city of Servius. (38)

Caligula goes to the Rhine. (39)

Julia and Agrippina exiled. (39)

Lucan (M. Annaeus Lucanus) (39-65) born. Latin poet. *De
Bello Civili°* or *Pharsalia* (*The Civil War*). (39)

39
CE

JEWISH AND CHRISTIAN HISTORY AND LITERATURE

40
CE

Agrippa I (Herod Agrippa), grandson of Herod the Great, King of Judea and Samaria, 40-44. (40)

Ignatius Theophorus (40-115) born. Syrian Greek Christian writer. Apostolic Father. Bishop of Antioch in Syria. Martyred in persecution of Christians during reign of Roman emperor Trajan. *Letter to the Ephesians°, Letter to the Magnesians°, Letter to the Traillians°, Letter to the Romans°, Letter to Polycarp°, Letter to the Philadelphians°, Letter to the Smyrnaeans°.* (40)

Clement of Rome (40-100) born. Roman Greek Christian writer. Apostolic Father. Leader in Roman churches. *I Clement°* (First Epistle of Clement of Rome to the Corinthians). (40)

Judea released from Roman procuratorial control from 41-44.(41)

Death of Agrippa I. (44)

Judea restored to procuratorial control for twenty years. (44)

Cuspius Fadus, Roman procurator of Judea, 44-46. (44)

Insurrection in Judea led by Theudas, false Messianic pretender. (45)

46
CE

Famine in Palestine. (46)

GRECO-ROMAN HISTORY AND LITERATURE

Gaius' expedition to the English channel. Gaius returns to Rome. Rebellion in Mauretania. Jewish representatives from Alexandria travel to Rome to protest treatment of Jews in Alexandria. Agrippa I receives Kingdom of Antipas. Judea restless. (40)   **40 CE**

Apollonius of Tyana (40-98) born. Itinerant Greek neo-Pythagorean philosopher and miracle worker. (40)

Martial (M. Valerius Martialis) (40-104) born. Latin poet. *Epigrammata°* (*Epigrams*). (40)

Quintilian (M. Fabius Quintilianus) (40-118) born. Latin rhetorician. *De Institutiones Oratoriae°* (*On the Education of the Orator*). (40)

Gaius murdered. Claudius becomes fourth Roman emperor and rules from 41 until his death in 54. Claudius resolves Alexandrine trouble. Judea and Samaria come under rule of Agrippa I. (41)

Agrippa I dies. Judea, again, made a province. (44)

Plutarch (45-120) born. Greek historian, biographer, and essayist. Authored several works. *Moralia°* (*Morals*) and *Bioi Paralleloi°* (*Parallel Lives*). (45)

Statius (Publius Papinus Statius) (45-96) born. Latin poet. Associate of Emperor Domitian. *Silvarum°* (*Silvae*), *Thebaidos°* (*Thebaid*), and *Achilleidos°* (*Achilleid*). (45)

45 CE

JEWISH AND CHRISTIAN HISTORY AND LITERATURE

46
CE

Philo Judeus, Alexandrian Jewish philosopher, dies. (46)

Tiberius Alexander, Roman procurator of Judea, 46-48. (46)

Paul the Apostle, Christian missionary and writer, in southern Galatia, 47-49. (47)

Ventidius Cumanus, Roman procurator in Judea, 48-52. (48)

Ananias, High Priest of Jews, 48-58. (48)

"Apostolic Council" in Jerusalem. (48)

Jews expelled from Rome by edict of Emperor Claudius. (49)

The Testaments of the Twelve Patriarchs° (50-100) written. (50)

Odes of Solomon° (50-150) written. (50)

Paul the Apostle, in Corinth, 51-53. (51)

I Thessalonians° (Paul) written. (52)

Antonius Felix, Roman procurator of Judea, 52-58. (52)

Paul the Apostle, in Ephesus and in Macedonia, 53-55. (53)

Roman military forces fight against Judean guerrillas, 54-66. (54)

54
CE

GRECO-ROMAN HISTORY AND LITERATURE

47
CE

Censorship of Claudius and L. Vitellius. Ludi Saeculares—
pageant of worship of state deities Apollo and Diana. (47)

Seneca the Younger called back to Rome; made tutor of Nero. (49)

Claudius adopts Nero as guardian of Britannicus. (50)

Dio Chrysostomus (Dio Cocceianus or Dio of Prusa) (50-130)
born. Greek rhetorician and sophist. *Discourses°*. (50)

During latter half of first century Roman soldiers, Asiatic
merchants, and Oriental slaves disseminate Mithraism
throughout the Empire.

Vespasian serves as consul. (51)

Gallio, proconsul in Achaea. (51-52)

Parthians occupy Armenia. (53)

Death of Claudius. Nero becomes fifth Roman emperor and
rules from 54 until his death in 68. Claudius deified. (54)

54
CE

JEWISH AND CHRISTIAN HISTORY AND LITERATURE

55   *I Corinthians°* (Paul) written. (55)
CE

Paul, again, in Corinth. (56)

Galatians° (Paul) and *II Corinthians°* (Paul) written. (56)

Paul arrested by Roman and Jewish authorities in Jerusalem. (58)

Romans° (Paul) written. (58)

Paul imprisoned in Caesarea, 58-60. (58)

Cn. Domitius Corbulo, Roman legate of Syria, 60-63. (60)

Porcius Festus, Roman procurator of Judea, 60-62. (60)

Paul is sent to Rome for trial. (60)

60
CE

GRECO-ROMAN HISTORY AND LITERATURE

Britannicus, son of Claudius, poisoned. (55)

Tacitus (Cornelius Tacitus) (55-120) born. Latin soldier, senator, colonial administrator, and historian. Proconsul of Asia, 112-113. *De Vita Agricolae° (Life of Agricola), Historiae° (The Histories), Annales De Moribus et Populis Germaniae° (Annals), Dialogus de Oratoribus° (Dialogue on Orators).* (55)

Epictetus (55-135) born. Phrygian Greek Stoic philosopher. Freedman. Probably expelled from Rome by Domitian in 89 along with other philosophers and religious figures. Later took up residence in Nicopolis in Epirus. His discourses, *Enchiridion°*, were preserved by Arrian. (55)

Nero refuses perpetual consulship. (58)

Nero murders his own mother, Agrippina, the fourth wife and niece of of Claudius. (59)

Nero introduces Greek games to Rome. (59)

Corbulo settles Armenia and serves as governor of Syria from 60-63. (60)

Festus becomes governor of Judea. (60)

JEWISH AND CHRISTIAN HISTORY AND LITERATURE

61
CE
Paul the Apostle is under house arrest in Rome, 61-63. (61)

Philippians° (Paul) and *Philemon°* (Paul) written. (62)

James, the brother of Jesus and head of Jewish Christian community in Jerusalem, is arrested and executed. (62)

Lucceius Albinus, Roman procurator of Judea, 62-64. (62)

Ananus II (son of Annas, Ananus I), High Priest of Jews. (62)

Gallus, Roman legate of Syria, 63-66. (63)

Peter and Paul executed in Rome by Romans. (64)

General persecution of Christians in Rome. (64)

Gessius Florus, Roman procurator of Judea, 64-66. (64)

Vespasian, Roman military commander, sent to Palestine to crush Jewish rebellion against Roman rule. (66)

Jewish Christians in Jerusalem flee to Pella in Transjordan. (66)

Mucianus, Roman legate of Syria, 67-69. (67)

Palestine is made an imperial Roman province. (67)

Vespasian, Roman legate of Palestine, 67-69. (67)

Vespasian besieges Jerusalem. (68)

68
CE
Qumran (Essene) community at Dead Sea is destroyed by Roman army. (68)

GRECO-ROMAN HISTORY AND LITERATURE

Pliny the Younger (C. Plinius Caecilius) (61-115) born.   **61**
Nephew of Pliny the Elder. Latin politician and rhetorician.   **CE**
Epistolae° (*The Letters*). (61)

Gallus serves as Roman legate of Syria from 63-66. (63)

Great fire in Rome. Christians persecuted. Construction of
Nero's palace. (64)

Conspiracy of Cn. Calpurnius Piso against Nero. (65)

Revolt in Palestine. (66)

Tiridates, Parthian ruler, crowned by Emperor Nero. Tiridates
worships Nero as Mithras. (66)

Cn. Domitius Corbulo, former legate of Syria, ordered to kill
himself. T. Flavius Vespasianus commands Roman troops in
Judea. Josephus, the Jewish historian, surrenders to
Vespasianus. (67)

Nero dies in June. Galba becomes sixth Roman emperor in the
autumn of same year but rules for less than a year. Vespasian
starts attack on Jerusalem. (68)

68
CE

JEWISH AND CHRISTIAN HISTORY AND LITERATURE

**69
CE**   Vespasian directs Titus, his eldest son, to lead Roman army in defeating remaining Jewish forces, while he returns to Rome to fight opponents. (69)

Polycarp of Smyrna (69-155) born. Asian Greek Christian theologian and writer. Apostolic Father. Bishop of Smyrna in Asia. Leader of the churches in Asia Minor. Martyred. *Epistle to the Philippians°*. (69)

Jerusalem falls to Roman forces of Titus. Titus rules for a brief period as Roman legate of Palestine; later Cerealis rules as Roman legate. Emperor Vespasian establishes special tax on Jews. (70)

Gospel of Mark°, written. (70)

The Jewish War° (Josephus) (70-90) written. (70)

Book of Biblical Antiquities° (Pseudo-Philo) written. (70)

II Baruch°, *IV Ezra°*, *III Baruch°*, *The Apocalypse of Abraham°* (70-120) written. (70)

Bassus, Roman legate of Palestine. (71)

Silva, Roman legate of Palestine, 72-80. (72)

**73
CE**   Romans destroy last Jewish resistance at Masada. (73)

GRECO-ROMAN HISTORY AND LITERATURE

Murder of Galba. Otho becomes seventh Roman emperor in January, but rules for only three months. Vitellius proclaimed emperor by Roman armies in Germany. (69)   **69 CE**

Otho defeated in battle; commits suicide in April. Vespasian's forces capture Rome; defeat Vitellius. Vespasian becomes eighth Roman emperor and rules from 69 until his death in 79. (69)

Suetonius (Gaius Suetonius Tranquillus) (69-130) born. Roman historian. Friend of Pliny the Younger with whom he corresponded. He eventually became secretary to Emperor Hadrian. *De Vita Caesarum°* (*Lives of the Caesars*), *De Viris Illustribus°*, (*The Lives of Illustrious Men*), and fragments concerning the lives of certain Roman authors. (69)

Vespasian arrives in Rome. (70)

Jerusalem falls to Roman legions of Titus, Vespasian's eldest son. (70)

Titus returns from Judea; given proconsular imperium; shares tribunician power with his father. Astrologers and philosophers expelled from Rome. (71)

Censorship of Vespasian and Titus. (73-74)   **73 CE**

JEWISH AND CHRISTIAN HISTORY AND LITERATURE

80
CE

Salvidemus, Roman legate of Palestine. (80)

Synagogue anathema against Jewish Christians (part of "Eighteen Benedictions"). (80)

James°, *Ephesians°*, *Colossians°*, *Matthew°*, *Luke-Acts°*, *Hebrews°*, *I Peter°* (80-100) written. (80)

Longinus, Roman governor of Palestine. (85)

Council of Rabbis at Jamnia. (90)

Revelation° (90-95) written. (90)

Gospel of John° and *Letters of John°* (90-110) written. (90)

90
CE

GRECO-ROMAN HISTORY AND LITERATURE

King Herod Agrippa II and his sister, Berenice, visit Rome. **75**
Berenice lives with Titus for some time in Rome. (75)   **CE**

Vespasian dies. Titus, his son, becomes ninth Roman emperor
and rules from 79 until his death in 81. Vesuvius erupts. (79)

Apollonius of Tyana, itinerant Greek neo-Pythagorean
philosopher and miracle-worker, active in Cappadocia.(80-98)

Death of Titus. Domitian becomes tenth Roman emperor and
rules from 81 until his death in 96. During his reign Domitian
creates a temple in Rome for Isis similar to the temple Caligula
constructed earlier on Campus Martius. From this period on Isis
and Serapis have the respect and official recognition of imperial
Roman dynasties. (81)

Triumph of Domitian over the Chatti, European tribe. (83)

Domitian becomes censor perpetuus. Legate of Moesia
defeated by Decebalus of Dacia. (85)

Ludi Saeculares. Dacians defeated. (88)

Domitian returns to Rome and triumphs. He issues edict against
astrologers and philosophers. (89)

JEWISH AND CHRISTIAN HISTORY AND LITERATURE

90
CE
    Persecution of Christians in Asia Minor and Rome, 90-96. (90)

Antiquities of the Jews° (Josephus) written. (93)

I Clement° (*First Epistle of Clement of Rome to the Corinthians*) written. (95)

Didache°, a manual of Christian discipline and practice and worship (95-140), written. (95)

Emperor Nerva rescinds Vespasian's tax on the Jews. (96)

Evaristus, Bishop of Rome, 100-109. (100)

100
CE
    Cerinthian heresy (denied full humanity of Jesus Christ). (100)

GRECO-ROMAN HISTORY AND LITERATURE

Arrian (Flavius Arrianus) (90-160) born. Bithynian Greek historian, politician, biographer, and soldier. Served as consul and legate of Cappadocia c. 135 under Emperor Hadrian and as consul under Antoninus Pius in 146. Defeated Alan invasion in 134. Pupil of Epictetus, the Stoic philosopher. He preserved the *Enchiridion° (Discourses) of Epictetus.* Authored *Anabaseos Alexandrou° (Anabasis of Alexander)*, historical, military and biographical texts about expedition of Alexander the Great, and *Indike° (Indica)*. (90)

90 CE

Domitian battles Sarmatae and Suevi, European tribes. (92)

Philosophers banished from Italy. (95)

Murder of Domitian. Nerva becomes eleventh Roman emperor and rules from 96 until his death in 98. (96)

Agrarian and social reform. (97)

Death of Nerva. Trajan becomes twelfth Roman emperor and rules from 98 until his death in 117. Tacitus is consul. (98)

Diogenes Laertius born. Greek historian. Lived sometime in 2nd century. *Philosophon Bioi° (Lives of the Philosophers).*

In the 2nd century the Dionysiac mysteries enjoyed a resurgence in Italy.

98 CE

JEWISH AND CHRISTIAN HISTORY AND LITERATURE

100 CE   *I and II Timothy°* and *Titus°* (100-120) written. (100)

Jude° (100-130) written. (100)

Justin Martyr (100-165) born. Samaritan Greek Christian theologian and writer. Apologist. Converted, 130. Taught in Ephesus and Rome. Martyred, 165. *First Apology°* (155), *Dialogue with Trypho the Jew°* (156), and *Second Apology°* (162) . (100)

Gospel of the Egyptians, The Apocryphon of James°, and *The Acts of John°* (100-150) written. (100)

Gospel of the Nazarenes and *Gospel of the Ebionites* (100-180) written. (100)

Gospel of Peter and *Sibylline Oracles°* (Christian portion) (100-200) written. (100)

Hermetica° (100-300) written. (100)

Letters° of Ignatius (105-115) written. (105)

Simeon of Jerusalem martyred. (107)

Alexander, Bishop of Rome, (109-119). (109)

110 CE   Persecution of Christians in Antioch. (110)

GRECO-ROMAN HISTORY AND LITERATURE

**101
CE**

First Dacian War. (101-102)

Chariton (sometime 2nd century) born. Greek novelist. Earliest of Greek novelists whose writings are extant. *Chaereas and Callirhoe°*.

Worship of Isis in southern Italy and Sicily in this period.

Second Dacian War. (105-106)

Arabia Petraea annexed. (106)

**106
CE**

JEWISH AND CHRISTIAN HISTORY AND LITERATURE

110
CE

Hermas° (110-140) written. (110)

Correspondence between Trajan, the Roman Emperor, and Pliny the Younger, a personal representative of the Emperor in Pontus and Bithynia (Asia Minor), about Christians (110-113). (110)

Christians persecuted in Bithynia (110-113). (110)

Jewish rebellions against Rome in Cyrenaica, Egypt, and Cyprus, 115-117. (115)

Sixtus I or Xystus, Bishop of Rome, 119-128. (119)

Basilides (active, 120-140). Alexandrian Greek Gnostic Christian theologian and apologist. Particularly influential in Egypt, 120-140. *Gospel, Commentary* and *Psalms* written. (120)

120
CE

GRECO-ROMAN HISTORY AND LITERATURE

111
CE

Pliny the Younger (C. Plinius Caecilius Secundus) sent to Bithynia in 111. Between 111-113 the Younger Pliny corresponded with Emperor Trajan. (111)

Tacitus proconsul of Asia. (112)

Trajan directs Parthian War. (113)

Annexation of Armenia. (114)

Annexation of Mesopotamia. Revolt of Jews in Cyrene. (115)

Alexander, son of Numenius, (115-140) active. Latin rhetorician and author of *Rhetores Graeci°*. (115)

Rebellion in East. Jewish rebellion spreads. (116)

Death of Trajan. Hadrian becomes thirteenth Roman emperor and rules from 117 until his death in 138. (117)

Hadrian arrives in Rome. (118)

Antoninus Pius becomes consul. (120)

Hadrian visits Western provinces. (121)

121
CE

JEWISH AND CHRISTIAN HISTORY AND LITERATURE

125
CE

Apology (Quadratus, Christian Apologist), written. This text was addressed to Roman emperor Hadrian. (125)

Letter of II Clement°, (125-150) and *The Paraleipomena of Jeremiah°* (the things omitted from Jeremiah) (125-150) written. (125?)

Gospel of Thomas° (125-150) written. (125)

Telesphorus, Bishop of Rome, 128-136. (128)

Epistle of Barnabas° and *Epistle of Diognetus°*, written. (130)

Apology° (Aristides) (130-140) written. (130)

II Peter° (130-150) written. (130)

Marcion of Pontus (active, 130-160). Asian Greek Gnostic Christian writer. Theological adversary of Irenaeus. Founder of Marcionite Church. *The Antitheses.* (130)

130
CE
Papias, Asian Greek Christian, active. Probably served as Bishop of Hierapolis.

GRECO-ROMAN HISTORY AND LITERATURE

Aurelius (Marcus Aurelius Antoninus) (121-180) born. Roman emperor, soldier, philosopher. His *Ton Eis Eauton°* *(Meditations)* reflect his devotion to Stoicism. (121)

121
CE

Hadrian in Britain. Moors revolt. (122).

Hadrian in Asia Minor. (124)

Apuleius (124-?) born. Latin novelist. He authored *Metamorphoses° (The Golden Ass)*, an early example of the Latin novel, and other extant works. (124)

Maximus of Tyre (125-185) born. Greek sophist and eclectic philosopher. Active during reign of Commodus. *Orationes°*. (125)

Hadrian in Athens. (129)

129
CE

JEWISH AND CHRISTIAN HISTORY AND LITERATURE

130
CE

Explanation of the Sayings of the Lord. (130)

Jewish rebellion in Palestine, led by Bar Cocheba (Bar Kokhba), 131-135. (131)

Valentinus, (active, 135-180). Alexandrian Greek Gnostic Christian theologian and apologist. Founder of sect known as "Valentinians". Influential Gnostic Christian, particularly, in Egypt, Cyprus, and Rome. (135)

Bar Cochba's (Bar Kokhba) Jewish rebellion suppressed. Jerusalem destroyed. Roman colony, Aelia Capitolina, built on site of city. Hadrian, Roman emperor, institutes anti-Jewish legislation. (135)

Hyginus, Bishop of Rome, 136-140. (136)

Marcion comes to Rome to try to influence the theological direction of Roman Christian community. (138)

Pius I, Bishop of Rome, 140-155. (140)

Persecution of Christians by Rome in Athens and Asia Minor. (140)

Irenaeus (140-200) born. Asian Greek Christian theologian and writer. Apologist. Became Bishop of Lyons in Gaul, 178. *Against the Heresies°* and *The Demonstration of the Apostolic Preaching°.* (140)

Marcion condemned by Church in Rome. Beginning of Marcionite Church. (144)

144
CE

GRECO-ROMAN HISTORY AND LITERATURE

**131
CE**

Jewish rebellion under Bar Cochba (Bar Kokhba). Rebellion lasts four years. (131)

Jewish rebellion suppressed. Hadrian destroys Jerusalem and builds Roman colony, Aelia Capitolina, on site of city. Political reorganization of Syria-Palestine. (135)

Hadrian adopts L. Aelius as Caesar. (136)

L. Aelius Caesar dies. Hadrian adopts Antoninus as co-regent. Hadrian dies. Antoninus Pius becomes fourteenth Roman emperor and rules from 138 until his death in 161. (138)

Marcus Aurelius becomes consul. (140)

Gaius, Latin jurist, active in reigns of Pius and Aurelius. He authored text on Roman Law, *Institutionum Commentarii°*.

Nine-hundredth anniversary of establishment of Rome. (148)

**148
CE**

JEWISH AND CHRISTIAN HISTORY AND LITERATURE

150
CE
Tatian (active, 150-190). Syrian Greek Christian theologian and writer. Apologist. Studied with Justin Martyr. Later became a gnostic and founded a sect (Encratites), 172. *The Word to the Gentiles°*. Edited *Diatessaron°* (150-180), a compilation of the life of Christ based on the four gospels which was used by Syriac-speaking churches until 5th century. (150)

Melito (active 150-190). Asian Greek Christian apologist. Served as Bishop of Sardes. *The Lord's Passion°*. (150)

Gospel of Philip°, *The Acts of Pilate°*, *The Dialogue of the Savior*, *The Protoevangelium of James°*, and *The Infancy Gospel of Thomas°* (150-200) written. (150)

Clement of Alexandria (Titus Flavius Clemens) (150-215) born. Alexandrian Greek Christian theologian and writer. Apologist. Master of Alexandrian Catechetical School. *Protrepticus° (Exhortation)°*, *Paedagogus° (Tutor)*, *Stromata° (Carpets)*. (150)

Epistle to the Philippians° (Polycarp, Bishop of Smyrna) (150-155) written. (150)

Epistula Apostolorum° (Dialogues of Jesus with His disciples after the Resurrection) (150-160) written. (150)

The Word to the Gentiles° (Tatian) written. (150)

Diatessaron° (Tatian) (150-180) written. (150)

Polycarp, Bishop of Smyrna, martyred. (155)

155
CE
Anicetus, Bishop of Rome, 155-166. (155)

GRECO-ROMAN HISTORY AND LITERATURE

152
CE

Settlement of conflict in Mauretania. (152)

Rebellion in Egypt. (152-153)

Dio Cassius (155-235) born. Bithynian Greek historian. Authored eighty-book history of Rome. Only books 36-54 extant, [which cover from wars of Lucullus to death of Agrippa in 10 BC]. *Romaike Historia°* (*Roman History*). (155)

155
CE

JEWISH AND CHRISTIAN HISTORY AND LITERATURE

155
CE

Montanus, Christian charismatic prophet, active in region of Phyrgia in Asia Minor, 155-170. (155)

Smyrnan church of Polycarp issues letter of martyrdom of Polycarp, *Martyrdom of Polycarp°*, 155-160. (155)

Tertullian (Quintus Septimius Florens Tertullianus) (155-220) born. African Latin Christian theologian and writer. Apologist. Converted in mid-life. Authored numerous treatises 195-220. Around 207 joined a Montanist Christian sect. *Ad Nationes° (To the Heathen) Apologeticum° (Apology)*, *De Testimonio Animae° (The Testimony of the Soul)*, *Adversus Judaeos° (Against the Jews)*, *Ad Scapulam° (To Scapula)*, *Adversus Marcionem° (Against Marcion)*, *De Anima° (On the Soul)*, *De Fuga in Persecutione° (Concerning Flight in Persecution)*, *De Praescriptione Haereticorum° (Against All Heresies)*, *Adversus Hermogenem° (Against Hermogenes)*, *Adversus Valentinianos° (Against Valentinus)*, *Scorpiace° (The Scorpion's Bite)*, *De Carne Christi° (The Flesh of Christ)*, *De Resurrectione Carnis° (The Resurrection of the Flesh)*, *Adversus Praxean° (Against Praxeas)*, *Ad Martyras° (To the Martyrs)*, *De Spectaculis° (On the Spectacles)*, *De Oratione° (On Prayer)*, *De Patientia° (Of Patience)*, *De Paenitentia° (On Repentance)*, *De Cultu Feminarum° (On Female Dress)*, *Ad Uxorem° (To His Wife)*, *De Exhortatione Castitatis° (On Exhortation to Chastity)*, *De Monogamia° (On Monogamy)*, *De Virginibus Velandis° (On the Veiling of Virgins)*, *De Corona Militis° (On the Soldier's Crown)*, *De Idololatria° (On Idolatry)*, *De Ieiunio Adversus Psychicos (On Fasting)*, and *De Pudicitia° (On Modesty)*, written. (155)

Militades (active, 160-170). Asian Greek Christian writer. Apologist. (160)

160
CE

GRECO-ROMAN HISTORY AND LITERATURE

**157
CE**

Romans fight Dacians. (157-158)

M. Aurelius and L. Verus designated consuls. (160)

**160
CE**

JEWISH AND CHRISTIAN HISTORY AND LITERATURE

160
CE   *Anti-Marcionite Prologues to the Gospels°* (prologues to Mark, Luke, and John. Probably originated in Roman Church) (160-180) written. (160)

Claudius Apollinaris (active, 160-180). Bishop of Hierapolis.

Justin, martyred in Rome. (165)

Soter, Bishop of Rome, 166-174. (166)

166
CE

GRECO-ROMAN HISTORY AND LITERATURE

161
CE

M. Aurelius (161-180)

Antoninus Pius dies. M. Aurelius (Marcus Aurelius Antoninus) and L. Verus become fifteenth and sixteenth Roman emperors in 161 and rule Rome together. L. Verus rules with Aurelius from 161 until his death in 169. M. Aurelius becomes sole emperor in 169. He continues to rule as emperor until his death in 180. (161)

Lucian (Lucianus) active in reign of Aurelius. Itinerant Greek philosopher and rhetorician; Sophist. *Dialogues°*.

Herodian (Aelius Herodianus) active in Rome during reign of Aurelius. Alexandrian Greek grammarian. Only fragments remain of his treatise on Greek accents, his largest work.

Armenia invaded by Parthians.   L. Verus sent to east. (162)

Armenia retaken. (163)

Great plague spreads throughout Empire from east to west. (165)

Plague in Rome. Marcomanni and Quadi push pass Danube and invade northern Italy. Dacia attacked by Iazyges. (167)

Romans wage war against Marcommanni, Quadi, and Sarmatae. (168-175)

M. Aurelius leads war on northern front.   L. Verus dies. (169)

169
CE

JEWISH AND CHRISTIAN HISTORY AND LITERATURE

**170
CE**

Hippolytus (170-235) born. Roman Greek Christian theologian and writer. Apologist. First anti-bishop. Martyred. Authored numerous treatises. *Philosophoumena°* (*Refutation of All Heresies*), *Syntagma* (*Against All Heresies*), *The Antichrist°*, *The Chronicle°*, *Commentary on Daniel°*, *The Apostolic Tradition°* and several small biblical commentaries written. (170)

The Acts of Carpus, Papylus, and Agathonice°, *The Acts of Justin and His Companions°* and *The Acts of the Martyrs of Scilli in Africa°* (170-200) written. (170)

Eleutherius, Bishop of Rome, 174-189. (174)

Persecution of Christians in Lyons and Vienna. (177)

Celsus, anti-Christian philosopher, publishes *True Discourse°* (a treatise against Christians). Most of this text is extant in Origen's *Contra Celsus.* (177)

Plea for the Christians° and *On the Resurrection of the Dead°* (Athenagoras of Athens) written. (177)

Irenaeus becomes Bishop of Lyons. (178)

To Autolycus° (Theophilus of Antioch) written. (180)

**180
CE**

GRECO-ROMAN HISTORY AND LITERATURE

**172
CE**

Defeat of Macromanni. Rebellion in Egypt. (172)

Defeat of Quadi.
M. Aurelius begins writing his *Meditations°*. (174)

Defeat of Iazyges.
M. Aurelius and Commodus in East. (175)

M. Aurelius and Commodus in Rome; triumph together. (176)

Commodus becomes consul. Mauretanians defeated. (177)

Trouble and rebellion along Danube. (178-180)

M. Aurelius and Commodus in northern part of Empire. (178)

Marcus Aurelius dies. Commodus becomes seventeenth Roman emperor and rules from 180 until his death in 192. Dacians, Quadi, Iazyges, and Vandals pacified. (180)

**180
CE**

JEWISH AND CHRISTIAN HISTORY AND LITERATURE

180
CE

Against the Heresies° (Irenaeus of Lyons) (180-190) written. (180)

Muratorian Fragment°, (180-200) written. This text is an ancient Christian list of canonical books. (180)

Persecution of Christians in Scilli in Africa. (180)

Sextus Julius Africanus (180-240) born. Judean Greek Christian theologian and writer. Apologist. Served in army of Septimius Severus, who later became Emperor. Studied in Alexandria. Associated with Origen. *Chronicles* and *Kestoi°* (*Embroideries*) written. (180)

The Acts of Apollonius° and *Letter of the Churches of Vienne and Lyons to the Churches of Asia and Phrygia°* (180-200) written. (180)

Origen (185-253) born. Alexandrian Greek Christian theologian and writer. Apologist. Succeeded Clement as master of Alexandrian Catechetical School. Excommunicated from Church of Alexandria. Later, master of Caesarean Catechetical School. He wrote more than any other Christian writer. *Contra Celsum°* (*Against Celsus*), *De Principiis°* (*First Principles*), *Discussion with Heraclides°*, *De Oratione°* (*On Prayer*), *Exhortatio ad Martyrium°* (*Exhortation to Martyrdom*) written. Several fragments of biblical literature (scholia and homilies) and letters and commentaries are also extant. (185)

Victor I, Bishop of Rome, 189-199. (189)

189
CE

Controversy ("quartodeciman") over date of Easter between Victor I and Polycrates. (189)

GRECO-ROMAN HISTORY AND LITERATURE

Maximus of Tyre active during reign of Commodus. Greek   **180**
Sophist and eclectic philosopher.   **CE**

During his reign Commodus was initiated into Mithraic religion. This religion continued to dominate religious life in the Roman empire for more than one hundred years.

Pertinax ends army rebellion in Britain. (186)

German rebellion ended. (188)

188
CE

JEWISH AND CHRISTIAN HISTORY AND LITERATURE

190   Alexandrian Catechetical School begun. Clement serves as
CE   master and teacher from 190-203. (190)

Novatian (190-260) born. Roman Latin Christian priest and
leader. Began schism out of protest against lenient
reconciliation for lapsed Christians in Roman church. Set
himself up as anti-Bishop in Rome against Bishop Cornelius.
This led to excommunication of Novatian and his party by
synod at Rome in 250, but his party survived. Novatianism was
an important Christian sect that lasted for several centuries. *De
Trinitate° (On the Trinity)*, *De Cibis Judaicis°* (On Jewish
Foods), *De Spectaculis (On Shows)*, *De Bono Pudicitiae° (On
the Advantage of Modesty)* written. (190)

Victor I, Bishop of Rome, condemns Montanist Christianity.
(196)
Edict of Severus, Emperor of Rome, forbids proselytizing by
Jews and Christians. (197)

199   Zephyrinus, Bishop of Rome, 199-217. (199)
CE

GRECO-ROMAN HISTORY AND LITERATURE

Pertinax ends disorders in Africa. (190)   **190**
                                                   CE

Commodus murdered. (192)

Pertinax becomes eighteenth Roman emperor (January); murdered (March). Julianus becomes nineteenth Roman emperor; killed (June). Septimius Severus becomes twentieth Roman emperor and rules from 193 until his death in 211. Clodius Albinus of Britain designated Caesar. Severus attacks Pescennius Niger whom Syrian legions had designated Emperor. Byzantium siege begins. (193)

Pescennius Niger defeated; dies. Severus pushes past Euphrates. (194)

Juvenal (Decimus Junius Juvenalis) active towards end of 2nd century. Roman satirist. *Saturae°* (*Satires*).

Caracalla designated Caesar. Byzantium falls. (196)

Albinus defeated. Severus returns to Rome and then continues campaign in East. (197)

Caracalla designated Augustus with Severus. (197-198)

                                                   197
                                                   CE

JEWISH AND CHRISTIAN HISTORY AND LITERATURE

200
CE Cyprian (Thascius Caecilius Cyprianus) (200-258) born. African Latin Christian theologian and writer. Apologist. Disciple of Tertullian. Became Bishop of Carthage, 249. Hid near Carthage during Decian persecution, 250. Returned to Carthage, 251. Banished by Roman authorities, 257. Martyred during Valerian persecution, 258. *De Lapsis° (Concerning the Lapsed), De Ecclesiae Unitate° (The Unity of the Church), De Opere et Eleemosynis° (Concerning Works and Almsgiving), De Bono Patientiae° (The Advantage of Patience), De Zelo et Livore° (Jealousy and Envy), Ad Fortunatum de Exhortatione Martyrii° (To Fortunatus: Exhortation to Martyrdom), Ad Donatum° (To Donatus), Testimoniorum Libri III ad Quirinum° (Three Books of Testimonies Against the Jews), De Dominica Oratione°, (On the Lord's Prayer)* and *De Habitu Virginum° (On the Dress of Virgins)* and numerous letters written. (200)

The Acts of Thomas° (200-300) written. (200)

Marcus Minucius Felix (active, 200-240). Roman Latin Christian lawyer and writer. Apologist. *Octavius°* written. (200)

Mishna°, a compilation of Jewish law, completed by Judah the Patriarch and the Rabbinical community. The *Mishna* is the first part of the Jewish *Talmud°*. Along with the Hebrew scriptures, the *Talmud* is the basis for Jewish life, practice, and thought. (200)

Christian Catechetical School in Alexandria closed. (202)

Clement escapes to Cappadocia. (202)

Persecution of Christians in Alexandria and North Africa begans. (202)

203
CE Christian Catechetical School in Alexandria reopened and directed by Origen, 203-231. (203)

GRECO-ROMAN HISTORY AND LITERATURE

Severus in Egypt and Syria. Later he travels to Danube. (199-200)   **199 CE**

Flavius Philostratus. Active around turn of century. Latin historian and philosopher. Authored several works including *Lives of the Sophists°* and *Life of Apollonius of Tyana °*.

Athenaeus. Active during reign of Septimius Severus. Greek grammarian. *Deipnosophistae°* (*The Sophists at Dinner*).

Severus issues edict against Christians. (202)

Geta, consul. (203)   **203 CE**

JEWISH AND CHRISTIAN HISTORY AND LITERATURE

203   Perpetua and Felicita, two Christian women, martyred in
CE   Carthage. (203)

Origen tutored by Ammonius Saccas, prominent Neoplatonic
philosopher in Alexandria, 205-210. (205)

Dionysius of Alexandria (205-265) born. Alexandrian Greek
Christian theologian and writer. Apologist. Pupil of Origen.
Bishop of Alexandria and master of Alexandrian Catechetical
School. Fled during persecution of Decius, Roman Emperor,
249. Returned to Alexandria after death of Decius, but was later
exiled by Roman authorities during reign of Emperor Valerian.
On Nature, On the Promise, and *Refutations and Apology*
written. (205)

Tertullian becomes a Montanist. (207)

Sabellius (active, 210). Christian theologian who advocates
modalistic Monarchian conception of Trinity.(210)

210
CE

GRECO-ROMAN HISTORY AND LITERATURE

Severus in Africa. (203-204)   **203**
                                                                 CE

Caracalla and Geta, consuls. (205)

Plotinus (205-262) born. Father of neo-Platonism. Porphyry
compiled his writings. *Enneads* °. (205)

Severus goes to Britain. (208)

Herodian (Herodianus). Active in the early and middle parts of
the third century. Syrian Greek historian. He authored a history
of the Roman emperors from the death of Marcus Aurelius to
Gordian III (180 CE-238 CE) entitled *History of the Emperors
From Marcus*°.

Septimius Severus dies. Geta and Caracalla go to Rome and
become twenty-first and twenty-second Roman emperors. (211)

Caracalla murders Geta. Caracalla rules as Roman emperor
until his death in 217. (212)

                                                                 212
                                                                 CE

JEWISH AND CHRISTIAN HISTORY AND LITERATURE

**213
CE**
Gregory Thaumaturgus, the Wonder Worker, (213-270) born. Asian Greek Christian theologian and writer. Apologist. Student of Origen in Caesarea. Bishop of Neocaesarea. *The Panegyric to Origen°, Symbol°, Canonical Epistle°*, and *To Theopompus on the Impossibility and Possibility of God°* written. (213)

Apostolic Tradition (Hippolytus), a Christian church order, written. (215)

Caracalla, Roman Emperor, loots Alexandria and closes Christian schools.

Origen, master of Alexandrian Catechetical School, goes to Caesarea. (216)

Sabellius condemned. (216)

Hippolytus attacks Sabellius and his adherents; argues for a subordinationist understanding of Christian doctrine of trinity. (217)

Calixtus I, Bishop of Rome, 217-222. (217)

Urban I, Bishop of Rome, 222-230. (222)

Clement of Alexandria excommunicated from Church of Alexandria by synod of churches at instigation of Demetrius, Bishop of Alexandria. (225)

**225
CE**

GRECO-ROMAN HISTORY AND LITERATURE

**215
CE**

Caracalla constructs temple to Isis on the Quirinal in the center of Rome. (215)

Caracalla in Antioch. (215-216)

Caracalla murdered in east. Macrinus becomes twenty-third Roman emperor and rules until his death in 218. (217)

Macrinus defeated and killed by supporters of Elagabalus. Elagabalus becomes twenty-fourth Roman emperor in 218 and rules until his death in 222. (218)

Elagabalus, consul. (220)

Elegabalus murdered. Severus Alexander becomes twenty-fifth Roman emperor and rules until his death in 235. (222)

Severus Alexander and Dio Cassius, consuls. (229)

**229
CE**

JEWISH AND CHRISTIAN HISTORY AND LITERATURE

230
CE

Pontian, Bishop of Rome, 230-235. (230)

Heraclas (Demetrius' successor), Bishop of Alexandria, excommunicates Origen from Church of Alexandria. Origen leaves for Caesarea. Under the authority of Bishop of Caesarea, Origen begins new school of theology in Caesarea which he directs for twenty years. (232)

Methodius (235-311) born. Asian Greek Christian theologian and writer. Apologist. Active in Asia Minor. Intellectual adversary of Origen. *The Symposium or On Virginity°*, *The Treatise on Free Will° On the Resurrection°* and *On Life and Reasonable Actions°* written. (235)

Maximinus Thrax, Roman Emperor, exiles Pontian, Bishop of Rome, and Hippolytus, anti-bishop, to Sardinia; Anterus, elected Bishop of Rome by Roman community. (235)

Hippolytus of Rome, dies. (235)

Fabian, Bishop of Rome, 236-250. (236)

236
CE

GRECO-ROMAN HISTORY AND LITERATURE

Persians invade Mesopotamia. (230)   **230**
                                                      CE
Severus Alexander campaigns in east; Persians defeat Romans.
(231-233)

Severus Alexander in Rome. (233)

Maximinus Thrax proclaimed emperor by Pannonian legions.
(234)

Severus Alexander dies. Maximinus Thrax becomes twenty-sixth Roman emperor in 235 and rules until 238. Edicts against Christians. (235)

Roman legions battle Dacians and Sarmatians. (236-237)

Mesopotamia invaded by Persians. (237-238)

Gordian I, proconsul of Africa, and Gordian II, his son, become twenty-seventh and twenty-eighth Roman emperors in 238 and rule together for a brief period. Gordian II killed by Numidian legate. Gordian I commits suicide. (238)

                                                      238
                                                      CE

JEWISH AND CHRISTIAN HISTORY AND LITERATURE

240
CE

Lactantius (Lucius Caecilius Firmianus Lactantius) (240-320) born. African Latin Christian theologian and writer. Apologist and poet. Originally appointed by Diocletian as a teacher of rhetoric at Nicomedia. After his conversion in 300 he was relieved of this position. Later, he served as tutor to the son of Roman Emperor Constantine. *Divinae Institutiones° (The Divine Institutes), De Opificio Dei° (The Workmanship of God), De Ira Dei° (The Anger of God), Epitome° (The Epitome of the Divine Institutes), De Mortibus Persecutorum° (Of The Manner In Which The Persecutors Died)* written. (240)

Mani (active, 242-275). Babylonian missionary and religious teacher. Created and proclaimed a new Persian syncretistic universal religion—Manichaeism—that consisted of elements of Buddhism, Zoroastrianism, and Christianity. Manichaeism lasted for centuries. It was a serious rival of Christianity in certain parts of Mediterranean region and Asia. Mani was crucified in 275. Mani established a church with both doctrine and scriptures. Augustine was a Manichaean for several years. (242)

Dionysius, Bishop of Alexandria, and master of Alexandrian Catechetical School, 248-265. (248)

248
CE

GRECO-ROMAN HISTORY AND LITERATURE

Balbinus and Pupienus appointed twenty-ninth and thirtieth emperors by Roman Senate in 238. They rule for a brief period. Maximinus Thrax, former emperor, killed. Balbinus and Pupienus killed by Praetorians who appoint Gordian III thirty-first Roman emperor. Gordian III rules from 238 to 244. Goths and Capri cross Danube in invasion. (238)   **238 CE**

Gordian III murdered. Philip, the Arabian, after settlement with Persians, becomes thirty-second Roman emperor in 244 and rules until 249. (244)

Fighting in Danube area. (245-247)

Philip, son of Emperor, designated Augustus. (247)

Decius resolves fighting in Pannonia and Moesia. (248)

248 CE

JEWISH AND CHRISTIAN HISTORY AND LITERATURE

249
CE
Decius, Roman Emperor, issues edict of persecution against Christians. This affects Christians throughout the empire and results in death of thousands of Christians, 249-251. (249)

Cornelius, Bishop of Rome, 251-253. (251)

Roman church holds Synod on Novatian schism. (251)

Lucius I, Bishop of Rome, 253-254. (253)

Stephen I, Bishop of Rome, 254-257. (254)

Synod of Carthage. (256)

Sixtus I, Bishop of Rome, 257-258. (257)

Valerian, Roman Emperor, renews persecution of Christians throughout the Empire, 257-258. (257)

Denis, Bishop of Rome, 259-268. (259)

259
CE

GRECO-ROMAN HISTORY AND LITERATURE

Decius kills emperor Philip and his son in battle. Goths **249** continue fighting. Decius designated Roman emperor in 249 by **CE** his legions and rules until his death in 251. (249)

Period of persecution of Christians. (249-251)

Decius defeated and killed. Trebonianus Gallus becomes thirty-third Roman emperor in 251 and rules until 253. (251)

Northern frontier invaded by Goths and barbarians. Mesopotamia invaded by Persians. (252)

Aemilianus becomes thirty-fourth Roman emperor in 253 and rules for only a brief period. (253)

Trebonianus Gallus defeated and killed. Rhine legions designate Valerianus as emperor. Aemilianus killed by his own troops. Valerianus, and his son, Gallienus, become thirty-fifth and thirty-sixth Roman emperors in 253 and rule together until 260. Gallienus becomes sole ruler after 260. (253)

Goths attack Asia Minor. (256)

Valerianus begins persecution of Christians. (257)

General Bibliography of References

A. Individual Texts

Altaner, B., *Patrology* (New York, 1960) English Translation.

Barrett, C. K. (ed.), *The New Testament Background: Selected Documents* (New York, 1957).

Bauer, W., *Orthodoxy and Heresy in Earliest Christianity* (Philadelphia, 1971) English Translation.

Bickerman, E., *From Ezra to the Last of the Maccabees: Foundations of Post-Biblical Judaism* (New York, 1962).

Bickerman, E., *Chronology of the Ancient World* (Ithaca, 1968).

Cameron, R., *The Other Gospels* (Philadelphia, 1982).

Cary, M. and Scullard, H. H., *A History of Rome: Down to the Reign of Constantine* (New York, 1978).

Chadwick, H., *The Early Church* (Baltimore, 1967).

Charlesworth, J. H. (ed.), *The Old Testament Pseudepigrapha* (Garden City, 1983).

Charlesworth, M. P., *The Roman Empire* (Oxford, 1951).

Conzelmann, H., *History of Primitive Christianity* (Nashville, 1979) English Translation.

Cross, F. (ed.), *The Oxford Dictionary of the Christian Church* (London, 1957).

Cumont, F., *Oriental Religions in Roman Paganism* (New York, 1956) English Translation.

Foakes-Jackson, F. J. and Lake, K., *The Beginnings of Christianity* (London, 1920-1933).

Garnsey, P. and Saller, R., *The Roman Empire* (Berkeley and Los Angeles, 1987).

Garzetti, A., *From Tiberius to the Antonines* (London, 1974) English Translation.

Hammond, N. G. L. and Scullard, H. H. (eds.), *The Oxford Classical Dictionary* (Oxford, 1970).

Harnack, A., *Die Chronologie der Altchristlichen Literatur 2.* (Leipzig, 1904).

Harnack, A., *History of Dogma* (New York, 1961) English Translation.

Harnack, A., *The Mission and Expansion of Christianity* (London, 1908) English Translation.

Harvey, P., (ed.), *The Oxford Companion to Classical Literature* (Oxford, 1959).

Hennecke, E., *New Testament Apocrypha* (Philadelphia, 1963-1965) English Translation.

Jones, A. H. M., *The Decline of the Ancient World* (London and New York, 1978).

Jones, H. S., *Companion to Roman History* (Oxford, 1912).

Jones, H. S., *The Roman Empire* (London, 1916).

Koester, H., *Introduction to the New Testament* (Philadelphia and New York, 1982) English Translation.

Kummel, W. G., *Introduction to the New Testament* (Nashville and New York, 1975) English Translation.

Lange, N. De, *Apocrypha: Jewish Literature of the Hellenistic Age* (New York, 1978).

Leith, J. (ed.), *Creeds of the Churches* (Richmond, 1973).

Lewis, N. and Reinhold, M. (eds.), *Roman Civilization* (New York, 1966).

Lietzmann, H., *A History of the Early Church* (Cleveland, 1961) English Translation.

Mattingly, H., *Christianity in the Roman Empire* (New York and London, 1967).

Mattingly, H., *Roman Imperial Civilization* (Garden City, 1959).

Nickelsburg, G. W. E., *Jewish Literature Between the Bible and the Mishnah* (Philadelphia, 1981).

Nilsson, M. P., *Imperial Rome* (New York, 1962).

Parker, H. M. D., *A History of the Roman World from A.D. 138 to 337* (London, 1958).

Quasten, J., *Patrology* (Westminster, 1950-1960).

Ramsey, W. M., *The Church in the Roman Empire* (London, 1893).

Reicke, B., *The New Testament Era: The World of the Bible from 500 B.C. to A.D. 100* (Philadelphia, 1968) English Translation.

Robinson, J. M., (ed.), *The Nag Hammadi Library* (San Francisco, 1977).

Rost, L., *Judaism Outside the Hebrew Canon* (Nashville and New York, 1976) English Translation.

Rostovtzeff, M., *The Social and Economic History of the Hellenistic World* (Oxford, 1941).

Rostovtzeff, M., *The Social and Economic History of the Roman Empire* (Oxford, 1957).

Salmon, E. T., *A History of the Roman World from 30 B.C. to A.D. 138* (London, 1959).

Soggin, J. A., *Introduction to the Old Testament* (Philadelphia, 1976) English Translation.

Syme, R., *The Roman Revolution* (New York, 1979).

Vermes, G., *The Dead Sea Scrolls* (Cleveland, 1978).

Vermes, G., *The Dead Sea Scrolls in English* (New York, 1975).

Walker, W., *A History of the Christian Church* (New York, 1970).

B. Series

Baillie, J. and McNeill, J. T. and Van Dusen, H. P. (eds.), *The Library of Christian Classics* (Philadelphia, 1953-1969).

Coxe, A. C. (ed.), *The Ante-Nicene Fathers* (Grand Rapids, Mich., 1979).

Loeb, J. and Page, T. E. and others (eds.), *The Loeb Classical Library* (Cambridge and London, 1925-   ).

Quasten, J. and Plumpe, J. C. (eds.), *Ancient Christian Writers* (New York and Paramus, N. J., 1946-   ).

Schopp, L. and Deferrari, R. J. (eds.), *The Fathers of the Church* (Washington, D. C., 1947-   ).

Bibliography of English
Translations of Greco-Roman and Jewish
and Christian Literature

Greco-Roman Literature

Appian
White, H. (tr.), *Appian's Roman History*, four volumes (Cambridge and London, 1964). LCL *

Apuleius (Lucius Apuleius)
Adlington, W. and Gaselee, S. (trs.), *Apuleius: The Golden Ass* (Cambridge and London, 1965) LCL

Arrian (Flavius Arrianus)
Oldfather, W. A. (tr.), *Epictetus: The Discourses As Reported by Arrian*, two volumes (Cambridge and London, 1967) LCL

Robson, E. I. (tr.), *Arrian: Anabasis Alexandri and Indica*, two volumes (Cambridge and London, 1966). LCL

Athenaeus
Gulick, C. B. (tr.), *The Deipnosophists (The Sophists at Dinner)*, seven volumes (Cambridge and London, 1969. LCL

Aurelius (Marcus Aurelius Antoninus)
Haines, C. R. (tr), *The Communings With Himself of Marcus Aurelius Antoninus Emperor of Rome Together With His Speeches and Sayings* (Cambridge and London, 1961). LCL

Caesar (C. Julius Caesar)
Edward, H. J. (tr.), *Caesar: The Gallic War* (Cambridge and London). LCL

Peskett, A. G. (tr.), *Caesar: The Civil Wars* (Cambridge and London, 1966). LCL

* LCL -The Loeb Classical Library

Way, A. G. (tr.), *Caesar: Alexandrian, African, and Spanish Wars* Cambridge and London, 1964). LCL

As Way notes in the introduction of his translation, these works are no longer ascribed Julius Caesar. The author is unknown.

Cato (M. Porcius Cato)
Hooper, W. D. (tr.) *Marcus Porcius Cato on Agriculture* (Cambridge and London, 1954). LCL

Catullus (G. Valerius Catallus)
Cornish, F. W. and Postgate, J. P. (trs.) *Catullus, Tibullus and Pervigilium Veneris: The Poems* (Cambridge and London, 1935). LCL

Cicero (M. Tullius Cicero)
Rolfe, J. C. and Rackham, H. and Gardner, R. and others (trs.), *Cicero*, twenty-eight volumes (Cambridge and London, 1948-1967).

Dio Cassius
Cary, E. (tr.), *Dio's Roman History*, nine volumes (Cambridge and London, 1961). LCL

Dio Chrysostomus
Cohoon, J. W. and Crosby, H. L. (trs.), *Dio Chrysostom: Discourses*, five volumes (Cambridge and London, 1961). LCL

Diogenes Laertius
Hicks, R. D. (tr.), *Diogenes Laertius: Lives of Eminent Philosophers*, two volumes (Cambridge and London, 1950), LCL

Dionysius of Halicarnassus
Cary, E. (tr.), *The Roman Antiquities of Dionysius of Halicarnassus*, seven volumes (Cambridge and London, 1968). LCL

Epictetus
Oldfather, W. A. (tr.) *Epictetus: The Discourses As Reported By Arrian, The Manuel, And Fragments*, two volumes (Cambridge and London, 1967).LCL

Herodian (Herodianus)

Whittaker, C. R. (tr.), *Herodian: History of The Empire From The Time Of Marcus Aurelius*, two volumes (Cambridge and London, 1969). LCL

Horace (Q. Horatius Flaccus)

Fairclough, H. R. (tr.), *Horace: Satires, Epistles and Ars Poetica* (New York and London, 1926). LCL

Juvenal (D. Junius Juvenalis)

Ramsay, G. G. (tr.), *Juvenal and Persius: The Satires* (Cambridge and London, 1979). LCL

Livy (T. Livius)

Foster, B. O. et al. (trs.), *Livy: History*, fourteen volumes (Cambridge and London, 1963) LCL

Lucan (M. Annaeus Lucanus)

Duff, J. D. (tr.), *Lucan: Pharsalia* (Cambridge and London, 1962). LCL

Graves, R. (tr.), *Lucan: Pharsalia* (Baltimore, 1957).

Lucian (Lucianus)

Harmon, A. M. (tr.), *Lucian: Dialogues*, eight volumes (Cambridge and London, 1961). LCL

Lucretius (T. Lucretius Carus)

Rouse, W. H. D. (tr.), *Lucretius: De Rerum Natura* (Cambridge and London, 1938). LCL.

Martial (M. Valerius Martialis)

Ker, W. C. A. (tr.), *Martial: Epigrams*, two volumes (Cambridge and London, 1961-1968). LCL

Ovid (P. Ovidius Naso)

Frazer, J. G., *Ovid: Fasti* (Cambridge and London, 1976). LCL

Miller, F. J. (tr.), *Ovid: Metamorphoses*, two volumes (Cambridge and London, 1977). LCL

Mozley, J. H. (tr.), *Ovid: The Art of Love and Other Poems* (Cambridge and London, 1957). LCL

Showerman, G. (tr.), *Ovid: Heroides and Amores* (Cambridge and

London, 1971). LCL

Wheeler, A. L. (tr.), *Ovid: Tristia and Ex Ponto* (Cambridge and London 1965). LCL

Persius (A. Persius Flaccus)

Jenkinson, J. R. (tr.), *Persius: The Satires* (Warminster, England, 1980).

Ramsay, G. G. (tr.), *Juvenal and Persius: The Satires* (Cambridge and London, 1979). LCL

Philostratus (Flavius Philostratus)

Conybeare, F. C. (tr.), *Philostratus: The Life of Apollonius of Tyana*, two volumes (Cambridge and London, 1927)

Wright, W. C. (tr.), *Philostratus and Eunapius: The Lives of the Sophists* (Cambridge and London, 1968). LCL

Pliny the Younger (C. Plinius Caecilius)

Melmoth, W. (tr.), *Pliny: Letters*, two volumes (Cambridge and London, 1952). LCL

Pliny the Elder (C. Plinius Secundus)

Rackham, H. and Jones, W. H. S. and others (trs.), *Pliny: Natural History*, ten volumes (Cambridge and London, 1967). LCL

Plutarch

Babbitt,, F. C. and others (trs.), *Plutarch's Moralia*, fifteen volumes (Cambridge and London, 1960-1969). LCL

Perrin, B. (tr.), *Plutarch's Lives*, eleven volumes (Cambridge and London, 1959-1962). LCL

Polybius

Paton, W. R. (tr.), *Polybius: The Histories*, six volumes (Cambridge and London, 1954). LCL

Propertius (Sextus Propertius)

Butter, H. E. (tr.), *Propertius: The Elegies* (Cambridge and London, 1967). LCL

McCulloch, J. P. (tr.), *The Poems of Sextus Propertius* (Berkeley and London, 1974).

Quintilian (M. Fabius Quintilianus)
Butler, H. E. (tr.), *The Institutio Oratoria of Quintilian*, four volumes (Cambridge and London, 1953). LCL

Sallust (C. Sallustius Crispus)
Rolfe, J. C. (tr.), *Sallust: The War With Catiline and The War With Jugurtha* (Cambridge and London, 1965). LCL

Seneca the Younger (L. Annaeus Seneca)
Basore, J. W. (tr.), *Seneca: Moral Essays*, three volumes (Cambridge and London, 1970). LCL

Corcoran, T. H. (tr.), *Seneca: Naturales Quaestiones*, two volumes (Cambridge and London, 1979). LCL

Gummere, R. M. (tr.), *Seneca: Ad Lucilium Epistulae Morales*, three volumes (Cambridge and London, 1979). LCL

Miller, F. J. (tr.), *Seneca's Tragedies*, two volumes (Cambridge and and London, 1979). LCL

Seneca the Elder (M. Annaeus Seneca)
Winterbottom, M. (tr.), *The Elder Seneca: Controversies and The Suasoriae*, two volumes (Cambridge and London, 1974). LCL

Statius (Publius Papinus Statius)
Mozley, J. H. (tr.), *Statius: Silvae, Thebaid, and Achilleid*, two volumes (Cambridge and London, 1961-1967). LCL

Strabo
Jones, H. L. (tr.), *The Geography of Strabo*, eight volumes (Cambridge and London, 1969). LCL

Suetonius (G. Suetonius Tranquillus)
Adams, M. (ed.), *C. Suetonius Tranquillus: Divi August: Vita* (London and New York, 1959, Macmillan and St. Martin's Press).

Rolfe, J. C. (tr.), *Suetonius: The Lives of the Caesars*, two volumes (Cambridge and London, 1964-1965). LCL

Tacitus (Cornelius Tacitus)
Moore, C. H. and Jackson, J. (trs.), *Tacitus: The Histories and the Annals*, four volumes (Cambridge and London, 1931-1937). LCL

Terence (P. Terentius Afer)
Sargeaunt, J. (tr.), *Terence: The Lady of Andros, The Self-Tormentor, The Eunuch,* two volumes (Cambridge and London, 1964-1965). LCL

Tibullus (Albius Tibullus)
Cornish, F. W. and Postgate, J. P. (trs.), *Catullus, Tibullus, and Pervigilium Veneris: The Poems* (Cambridge and London, 1935). LCL

Varro (M. Terentius Varro)
Hooper, W. D. (tr.), *Marcus Terentius Varro On Agriculture* (Cambridge and London, 1954). LCL
Kent, R. G. (tr.), *Varro: On The Latin Language,* two volumes (Cambridge and London, 1954). LCL

Velleius (C. Velleius Paterculus)
Shipley, F. W. (tr.), *The Roman History of C. Velleius Paterculus* (Cambridge and London, 1961). LCL

Virgil (P. Vergilius Maro)
Fairclough, H. R. (tr.), *Vergil: Ecologues, Georgies, The Aeneid, and Minor Poems* two volumes (New York and London, 1932). LCL

Jewish Literature

Hebrew Canon (The Old Testament)
Dodd, C. H., Driver, G. and McHardy, W. D. (eds.) *The New York English Bible* (Cambridge, 1972).
Hirsch, S. R. (tr.), *The Pentateuch* (New York, 1986) English Translation.
May, H. G. and Metzger, B. M. (eds.), *The New Oxford Annotated Bible With The Apocrypha* (New York, 1973).
Orlinsky, H. M. (ed.), *Tanakh* (Philadelphia, New York, and Jerusalem,1985).

Qumran, Dead Sea, Essene Literature

Gaster, T. H. (tr.), *The Dead Sea Scriptures* (Garden City, 1956).

Vermes, G. (tr.), *The Dead Sea Scrolls in English* (New York, 1979).

Jewish Apocrypha and Pseudepigrapha

Charles, R. H. (ed.), *The Apocrypha and Pseudepigrapha of The Old Testament in English*, two volumes (Oxford, 1913)

Charlesworth, J. H. (ed.), *The Old Testament Pseudepigrapha*, two volumes (Garden City, 1983).

Jones, A. (ed.), *The Jerusalem Bible* (Garden City, 1968).

May, H. G. and Metzger, B. M. (eds.), *The New Oxford Annotated Bible With The Apocrypha* (New York, 1973).

Philo

Colson, F. H. and Whitaker, G. H. (trs.), *Philo*, twelve volumes (Cambridge and London, 1968). LCL *

Josephus

Thackeray, H. S. J. and Marcus, R. (trs.), *Josephus*, nine volumes (Cambridge and London, 1976). LCL

Rabbinical Literature

Neusner, J. (tr.), *The Mishnah* (New Haven and London, 1988).

Christian Literature

The Christian Testament (The New Testament)

Dodd, C. H., Driver, G., and McHardy, W. D. (eds.) *The English Bible* (Cambridge, 1972).

Jones, A. (ed.), *The Jerusalem Bible* (Garden City, 1968).

May, H. G. and Metzger, B. M. (eds.), *The New Oxford Annotated Bible With The Apocrypha* (New York, 1973).

The Apostolic Fathers

Coxe, A. C. (ed.), *The Apostolic Fathers* (Grand Rapids, Mich.,

* LCL -The Loeb Classical Library

1979) ANF *

Glimm, F. X., Marique, J. M. F., and Walsh, G. G. (trs.), *The Apostolic Fathers* (Washington, D. C., 1969) FOC *

Goodspeed, E. J. (tr.), *The Apostolic Fathers* (New York, 1950).

Kleist, J. A. (tr.), *The Epistles of St. Clement of Rome and St. Ignatius of Antioch* (New York and Ramsey, N. J., 1946) ACW *

_____, *The Didache, The Epistle of Barnabas, The Epistles and the Martyrdom of St. Polycarp, The Fragments of Papias, The Epistle of Diognetus* (New York and Ramsey, N. J., 1948) ACW

Lake, K. (tr.), *The Apostolic Fathers*, two volumes (Cambridge and London, 1977). LCL *

THE APOLOGISTS

Aristides

Coxe, A. C. (ed.), *Original Supplement: Peter, Tatian, Commentary of Origen and others* (Grand Rapids, Mich., 1979) ANF

Athenagoras

Coxe, A. C. (ed.), *Fathers of the Second Century* (Grand Rapids, Mich., 1979) ANF

Crehan, J. H. (tr.), *Athenagoras* (New York and Ramsey, N. J., 1955) ACW

Clement of Alexandria

Butterworth, G. W. (tr.), *Clement of Alexandria* (Cambridge and London, 1982). LCL

Coxe, A. C. (ed.), *Fathers of the Second Century* (Grand Rapids, Mich., 1979) ANF

Wood, S. P. (tr.), *Clement of Alexandria* (New York, 1954) FOC

Cyprian

Bevenot, M. (tr.), *St. Cyprian* (Westminster, Md. and London, 1957) ACW

Coxe, A. C. (ed.), *Hippolytus, Cyprian, Caius and Novation* (Grand Rapids, Mich., 1979) ANF

* ANF - The Ante-Nicene Fathers
* FOC - The Fathers of the Church
* ACW - Ancient Christian Writers
* LCL - The Loeb Classical Library

Deferrari, R. J. (tr.), *Saint Cyprian: Treatises* (New York, 1958) FOC

Donna, R. B. (tr.), *Saint Cyprian: Letters 1-81* (Washington, D. C., 1981) FOC

Dionysius

Coxe, A. C. (ed.), *Gregory Thaumaturgus, Dionysius the Great, Julius Africanus, Anatolius and Methodius* (Grand Rapids, Mich., 1979) ANF

Minucius Felix

Arbesmann, R. (tr.), *Tertullian and Minucius Felix* (New York, 1950) FOC

Clark, G. W. (tr.), *The Octavius of Marcus Minucius Felix* (New York and Paramus, N. J., 1974) ACW

Coxe, A. C. (ed.), *Tertullian, Minucius Felix, Commodian, and Origen* (Grand Rapids, Mich., 1979) ANF

Gregory Thaumaturgus, the Wonder Worker

Coxe, A. C. (ed.), *Gregory Thaumaturgus, Dionysius the Great, Julius Africanus, Anatolius, and Methodius* (Grand Rapids, Mich., 1979) ANF

Hippolytus

Coxe, A. C. (ed.), *Hippolytus, Cyprian, Cains, and Novatian* (Grand Rapids, Mich., 1979) ANF

Irenaeus

Coxe, A. C. (ed.), *The Apostolic Fathers* (Grand Rapids, Mich. 1979) ANF

Smith, J. P. (tr.), *St. Irenaeus: Proof of the Apostolic Preaching* (Westminster, M. D. and London, 1952) ACW

Sextus Julius Africanus

Coxe, A. C. (ed.), *Gregory Thaumaturgus, Dionysius the Great, Julius Africanus, Anatolius and Methodius* (Grand Rapids, Mich., 1979) ANF

Justin Martyr

Coxe, A. C. (ed.), *The Apostolic Fathers* (Grand Rapids, Mich.,1979) ANF

Falls, T. B. (tr.), *Saint Justin Martyr* (New York, 1948) FOC

Lactantius

Coxe, A. C. (ed.), Lactantius, *Venantius, Asterius, Victorinus, Dionysius, Apostolic Teaching and Constitutions* (Grand Rapids, Mich., 1979) ANF

McDonald, M. F. (tr.), *Lactantius: The Divine Institutes* (Washington, D. C., 1981) FOC

_____, *Lactantius: The Minor Works* (Washington, D. C., 1965) FOC

Melito

Bonner, C. (tr.), *Melito of Sardes: The Homily on the Passion* (London, 1940).

Methodius

Coxe, A. C. (ed.), *Gregory Thaumaturgus, Dionysius the Great, Julius Africanus, Anatolius, and Methodius* (Grand Rapids, Mich., 1979) ANF

Musurillo, H. (tr.), *St. Methodius* (Westminster, Md. and London, 1958) ACW

Novatian

Coxe, A. C. (ed.), *Hippolytus, Cyprian, Caius, and Novatian* (Grand Rapids, Mich., 1979) ANF

DeSimone, R. J. (tr.), *Novatian* (Washington, D. C. 1981) FOC

Origen

Coxe, A. C. (ed.), *Tertullian, Minucius Felix, Commodian, and Origen* (Grand Rapids, Mich., 1979) ANF

_____, *Original Supplement: Peter, Tatian, Commentary of Origen and others* (Grand Rapids, Mich., 1979) ANF

Lawson, R. P. (tr.), *Origen: The Song of Songs and Commentary and Homilies* (Westminster, Md. and London, 1957) ACW

O'Meara, J. J. (tr.), *Origen: Prayer and Exhortation to Martyrdom* (Westminster, Md. and London, 1954) ACW

Tatian

Coxe, A. C. (ed.), *Fathers of the Second Century* (Grand Rapids,

Mich., 1979) ANF

_____ (ed.), *Original Supplement: Peter, Tatian, Commentary of Origen* (Grand Rapids, Mich., 1979) ANF

Tertullian

Arbesmann, R., Daly, E. J., and Quain, E. A. (trs.) *Tertullian: Disciplinary, Moral and Ascetical Works* (New York, 1959) FOC

Coxe, A. C. (ed.), *Latin Christianity: Its Founder, Tertullian* (Grand Rapids, Mich., 1979) ANF

_____, *Tertullian, Minucius Felix, Commodian, and Origen* (Grand Rapids, Mich., 1979) ANF

Daly, E. J. (tr.), *Tertullian: Apology* (New York, 1950) FOC

LeSaint, W. P. (tr.), *Tertullian: Treatises on Marriage and Remarriage* (New York and Ramsey, N. J., 1951) ACW

Tertullian: Treatises on Penance (Westminster, Md. and London, 1959) ACW

Waszink, J. H. (tr.), *Tertullian: The Treatise Against Hermogenes* (Westminster, Md. and London, 1956) ACW

Theophilus

Coxe, A. C. (ed.), *Fathers of the Second Century* (Grand Rapids, Mich., 1979) ANF

Christian Apocrypha

Cameron, R. (ed.), *The Other Gospels* (Philadelphia, 1982).

Coxe, A. C. (ed.), *Original Supplement: Peter, Tatian, Commentary of Origen and others* (Grand Rapids, Mich., 1979) ANF

_____, *The Twelve Patriarchs, Excerpts and Epistles, and Apocrypha* (Grand Rapids, Mich., 1979). ANF

James, M. R. (tr.), *The Apocryphal New Testament, Being the Apocryphal Gospels, Acts, Epistles, and Apocalypses* (Oxford, 1960).

Schneemelcher, W. and Hennecke, E. (eds.), *New Testament Apocrypha* two volumes (Philadelphia, 1963 and 1965).

Gnostic Christian Literature

Cameron, R. (ed.), *The Other Gospels* (Philadelphia, 1982).

James, M. R. (tr.), *The Apocryphal New Testament, Being The Apocryphal Gospels, Acts, Epistles, and Apocalypses* (Oxford, 1960).

Robinson, J. and Meyer, M. W. (eds.), *The Nag Hammadi Library* (New York, 1981).

Index of Literature

A

Ab Urbe Condita (From the Founding of the City) – Livy, 23
Achilleid (Achilleidos) – Statius, 43
Acts of Apollonius, The, 72
Acts of Carpus, Papylus and Agathonice, The, 70
Acts of John, 56
Acts of Justin and His Companions, The, 70
Acts of the Martyrs of Scilli in Africa, The, 70
Acts of Pilate, The, 64
Acts of Thomas, The, 76
Advantage of Modesty, The (De Bono Pudicitiae) – Novatian, 74
Advantage of Patience, The (De Bono Patientiae) – Cyprian, 76
Aeneid, The –, Virgil, 19
African War, The (De Bello Africa) – Julius Caesar, 15
Against All Heresies (Syntagma) – Hippolytus, 70
Against All Heresies (De Praescriptione Haereticorum) – Tertullian, 66
Against Apion – Josephus, 40
Against Celsus (Contra Celsum) – Origen, 72
Against Flaccus – Philo, 30
Against the Heresies – Irenaeus, 62, 72
Against Hermogenes (Adversus Hermogenem) – Tertullian, 66
Against the Jews (Testimoniorum Libri III Ad Quirinum) – Cyprian, 76
Against the Jews (Adversus Judaeos) – Tertullian, 66
Against Marcion (Adversus Marcionem) – Tertullian, 66
Against Praxeas (Adversus Praxean) – Tertullian, 66
Against Valentinus (Adversus Valentinianos) – Tertullian, 66
Agriculture (De Agri Cultura) – Cato, 17
Agriculture (De Re Rustica) – Varro, 13
Alexandrian War, The (De Bello Alexandrino) – Julius Caesar, 15
Alexander or On the Question Whether Dumb Animals Have the Power of Reason – Philo, 30
Allegory of the Jewish Law – Philo, 30
Amores – Ovid, 27
Anabasis of Alexander (Anabaseos Alexandrou) – Arrian, 55
Andria (The Lady of Andros) – P. Terentius Afer, 3
Anger of God, The (De Ira Dei) – Lactantius, 84
Annals (Annales De Moribus et Populis Germaniae) – Tacitus, 47

Index of Persons

Biographical Sketch

PHILIP WALKER JACOBS was born in Cirencester, England. He has studied at Southern Illinois University, Union Theological Seminary in Virginia, and the University of Virginia, and holds degrees in Administration of Justice, Speech, Divinity, and New Testament and Early Christianity. He has taught at Iowa State University and served as a teaching assistant at the University of Virginia.

He is an ordained Presbyterian minister and has served churches in Virginia, New Jersey, and Louisiana, and Kentucky. He is presently working on his second book.